What they're say

As an entrepreneur who has helped hundreds grow businesses, I am often asked, "What is the difference between successful business owners and unsuccessful ones?" My number one answer has always been attitude—specifically, a can-do, positive attitude that is required to succeed, as well as discipline and many other characteristics. But the foundation is gratitude and attitude.

Doc Rock does a great job of creating a theme and an easy-to-remember approach to having a positive attitude every day. We make our best decisions when we are in a good frame of mind. Typically, costly decisions are made when we are overwhelmed with sadness or stress. As Doc so properly describes, this not only impacts our overall success, but our quality of life.

It's Terrific Tuesday as I write this. How awesome is that? Words have power, and if we can go around and remind people of what's great about the day we are living, we'll have an edge up on everything we do.

Todd Hopkins
Founder of Office Pride
International best-selling author of
The Janitor and *Stop Using the "B" Word*

Doc Rock provides excellent principles to assist us every day of the week. Each day is truly a gift which becomes our "Best Day Ever." There are *No Bad Days*, maybe a few bad minutes, and we need to constantly focus on our vision because we can never go where we cannot accept.

Joe Newberry
President/CEO
Redstone Federal Credit Union

NO BAD DAYS

SEIZE YOUR OPPORTUNITY

DR. KAROCKAS "DOC ROCK" WATKINS

No Bad Days
by Dr. Karockas Watkins
© 2022 by Dr. Karockas Watkins. All rights reserved.

Editing by Adam Colwell's WriteWorks, LLC, Adam Colwell and Ginger Colwell
Cover and interior design by Clarity Designworks
Published by Dr. Karockas Watkins through IngramSpark

Printed in the United States of America

ISBN (Paperback): 979-8-9864882-6-4
ISBN (Hardcover): 979-8-9900002-4-7
ISBN (eBook): 979-8-9864882-7-1

All rights reserved. Except in the case of brief quotations embodied in critical articles and reviews, no portion of this book may be reproduced, stored in a retrieval system, or transmitted in any form or by any means—electronic, mechanical, photocopy, recording, scanning, or other—without the prior written permission from the author. None of the material in this book may be reproduced for any commercial promotion, advertising or sale of a product or service.

While the author has made every effort to provide accurate internet addresses at the time of publication, neither the publisher nor the author assumes any responsibility for errors or for changes that occur after publication. Further, the publisher does not have any control over and does not assume any responsibility for author or third-party websites or their content.

CONTENTS

Acknowledgements vii
Every Day Matters! ix

Chapter 1: Super Sunday—Vision 1
Chapter 2: Marvelous Monday—Attitude 23
Chapter 3: Terrific Tuesday—Belief 41
Chapter 4: Wonderful Wednesday—Potential 55
Chapter 5: Triumphant Thursday—Confidence 75
Chapter 6: Fantastic Friday—Enthusiasm and Drive 91
Chapter 7: Successful Saturday—Purpose 105

Don't Wait for Tomorrow! 123
Endnotes 125

ACKNOWLEDGEMENTS

I would like to express my gratitude to my wonderful wife, Audra. Your support, love, and understanding are such a blessing to me. You know how to keep everything glued together in every situation. Thanks, too, to my three awesome kids, Brianna, Christian, and Joshua. Keep shooting for the galaxy! Maybe you will land on the moon.

Thanks to the leadership teams at Ability Plus Inc., Emmanuel The Connection Church, and Vision Excellence Company. Because of you, I get to put many leadership principles into action.

Additionally, thanks again to my editor and writing coach, Adam Colwell. Your focus and encouragement go a long way.

EVERY DAY MATTERS!

Do you wake up and wonder how the day is going to go? It is easy to accept the normal expectation for small or average results. You may allow little things to stop you from achieving your best in a given day. At the same time, there are people who seem to be offended, and think you positively strange, when you have an overly positive disposition.

Author Edmond Mbiaka is quoted as saying, "Every single day is a good day, no matter how bright or dark it is, because it always brings an opportunity to start a positive beginning in your life." Your day is not to be shaped by the external things that happen as it progresses, but by the internal vision you have as you go about that day. Many people rely on *things* to make their day a good one, but oftentimes, the things that make up your day are a byproduct of your understanding and inner thoughts.

I acted upon this truth when I found myself in a new executive position at a large not-for-profit organization. We went through a major period of transition, and they were challenging times. As I found myself struggling with motivation for myself and for my management team—I decided to do something about it.

Inspired by the biblical exhortations in Philippians 4, I began telling myself one thing at the start of every day.

There are no bad days.

As a Christian, I believed that God created each day to live to my fullest. I knew God wanted me to rejoice and be glad about the opportunities that came with each day. So, from that moment forward, I chose to never give in to disappointment and be sorry for an entire day.

Then I matched my attitude with a response. I gave each day a special name that I call, sign, and profess. For example, I call Sunday "Super Sunday." I sign it by using "Super Sunday" in my electronic messages. I profess it by saying "It's a Super Sunday" aloud throughout the day.

I also came up with the following:

- Marvelous Monday
- Terrific Tuesday
- Wonderful Wednesday
- Triumphant Thursday
- Fantastic Friday
- Successful Saturday

To be honest, these started out as nothing more than titles, but I have since developed attributes, characteristics, and principles to go with each one. As a result, my self-motivation technique has become a powerful way to motivate others—one that I unfold for you in this book.

At the foundation of *No Bad Days* is the idea of **self-motivation**, which I define as the ability to stir yourself to do what needs to be done without influence from other people. I recall a time when many of my company's managers were settling for merely meeting industry standards for how we serve our clients: middle-aged men and women with some

> At the foundation of *No Bad Days* is the idea of **self-motivation**.

sort of intellectual disability. I wanted us to do more than simply engage our clients to learn.

So, I took it upon myself to reach deep within and challenge all of us to come up with new approaches that took existing industry standards to a whole new level. We brought in people to teach art and music therapy. We started an entrepreneurship program where our clients could discover how to maximize their gifts. We found out their passions and worked on how we could help them perfect those passions. We even changed the branding of the company to indicate the extra level of services we were providing. In no time, our company *became* the industry leader in our field. More than that, our clients' lives were being enhanced.

········

Another word for self-motivation is **intrinsic motivation**. Intrinsic motivation involves engaging in a behavior because it is personally rewarding, enjoyable, or interesting, doing it for *its own sake* rather than from some external pressure or for an external reward. The behavior itself is its own reward.

It's been said that basketball legend Michael Jordan never played against others, but against himself. He was intrinsically motivated, and that motivation led him to become what many consider to be the greatest basketball player of all time. A practical example of intrinsic motivation is taking on more responsibility at work because you want to be challenged, and you enjoy the feeling of accomplishment it brings, rather than doing it to get a raise or a promotion. Another example is learning a new language because you like experiencing new things, not because your job requires it.

Essential to developing your intrinsic motivation is knowing your "why." In my book *God-A-Tude*, I talk about your why as being the reason you exist—your purpose for living. I tell people that their why is that thing that will get them out of bed when everyone else is still hitting the snooze button. When you discover your why, you will search diligently to recognize how to accomplish it, and you will wait as long as it takes to gain the knowledge, stability, and experience to fulfill it. To discover your why, ask yourself questions such as, "What is my passion?" "What comes easy to me?" "What excites me?" Your why shouldn't be something that is done just for money, because when you find your passion and it informs your purpose, you'll never "work" a day in your life.

Another key to your intrinsic motivation is having a circle of safety. You will function better, and innovation will be stirred within you, when you are in a safe environment. Your circle of safety also serves as your accountability group, allowing you to get up each morning, dream, and be motivated to take chances because you know that if you fail, your group will not judge you according to that failure.

I've identified seven factors of intrinsic motivation.

1. Curiosity pushes you to explore and learn for the sole pleasure of learning and mastering. In her article, "The Importance of Being Curious," leadership expert Dalia Molokhia shares about how being curious by putting herself in her young daughters' shoes as she learned new things has helped her as a mother. When you are curious, you open yourself to new information. In his Harvard Business Review article, "Why Curious People Are Destined for the C-Suite," Warren Berger told of the time when Dell Technologies founder, chairman, and CEO Michael Dell was asked in a PwC survey to name a trait that would most help chief executive officers succeed. Dell's response: "I would place my bet on curiosity."

2. Being **challenged** helps you work at a continuously optimal level toward meaningful goals to maximize your potential. As a CEO, I was once challenged, during an executive board meeting, with an aggressive goal to increase the number of clients we serve by three times more than the industry standard. The colleague said, "Doc Rock, I feel you and your team can do much more than this." Even though the colleague was a friend, it felt like an attack and one where I was being set up for failure. After gathering myself and realizing that he was challenging me to go beyond what I thought I could do, I asked myself, "Why am I looking to industry criteria to define what I can and can't do? I *can* do better, so let me be who I know I am." Within a year, we not only met the goal, but exceeded the industry standard for new client acquisitions by almost five times the amount.

3. Control comes from your basic desire to impact what happens and make decisions that affect the outcome. There was an executive who had to take control of a very politicized situation facing his company regarding cultural diversity. Disunity and strife within the community that the organization served was having a detrimental impact on many business leaders and their stakeholders. It resulted in some heated exchanges around the boardroom table, but the executive proactively worked to help everyone to see beyond their personal opinions and prejudices and to look at the situation in a positive manner. As a result, the leadership team was able to determine a proper organizational response, and everyone was motivated to stay the course.

4. You possess an innate need to be **complimented** and to see that you are appreciated and that your efforts are confirmed. Some people act as if they don't need to be complimented, but it is helpful, if only for the purpose of motivation. One of my dear colleagues who is a self-starter and a very disciplined person once admitted that while he was in college, he felt much better after he was complimented on the work he was doing as president of one of the student body clubs. He said the compliment served as additional fuel to fire his success by helping him accomplish more than he would have without the encouragement.

5. Cooperating with others satisfies your need for belonging. You also feel personal satisfaction when you help others and work together with them to achieve a shared goal. While serving on a board for a local branch of the YMCA (Young Men's Christian Association), I worked with the executive director on his vision and goals for the branch. We talked to potential donors together and formed several strategies, and it felt absolutely great to team up with such a talented individual. Not only did he encourage me, but he offered a higher level of insight that told me we couldn't do it alone and that we were better together. It is not about taking credit or having your name out there. It is about the cooperation of a team that satisfies your need to belong.

6. Competition poses a challenge and increases the importance you place on doing well. There was a time that I had two mid-level managers who were in competition for a new position we were creating in the company. Both came to me requesting to compete for the opening so that they could be motivated to rise to their best leadership skills and behavior. So, I went and observed them as they worked with individuals within their current departments, had meetings, and set goals. I gave them a level playing field, and the competition between the two was friendly yet determined. In the end, one rose to the top, but both learned, grew, and thrived. It was a really good process.

7. Using the **canvas** of your imagination stimulates your behavior as you use it to draw upon mental or virtual images. I have always said that if you can see something on the canvas of your imagination, you can have it! I discovered this to be true for myself when our company faced a difficult season. Everything looked bleak and problematic, but I had to visualize us doing well and becoming a great company within our industry. When I got to the office each day, I had some quiet time in which I pictured us succeeding, responding to crises, and being financially sound. I envisioned us talking to our clients so that they became partners with us. I saw us with smiles on our faces and receiving awards for our work. I told everyone what I saw and what I believed we could be, then we had meetings on how we could get there and put strategies in place to make things happen.

Within just two weeks, things started to change, and in six months, we had everything turned around! Visualizing was the initial dynamic, then my actions toward my team, as well as toward my own responsibilities, began to manifest what I was visualizing.

·······

Of course, self-motivated people are also enthusiastic. They have the ability to complete a task even in the face of barriers. There was a time at General Motors when I had to assist in the completion of a project with an aggressive two week deadline. My team and I decided to make it a fun challenge. As engineers, we began by encouraging those on the production line to let us help them to troubleshoot the problems and teach us what we missed. "Tomorrow, we are going to be able to test five parts," I said, "then, the next day, we are going to test ten parts. Who is going to be the person who leads the team today?" No one wanted to let us down. Despite hard work and long hours, our shared enthusiasm drove us to complete the task on deadline and with excellence. It was all a matter of changing our mindset about the task from being an overwhelming and difficult burden to an enjoyable responsibility that we did together. That made the project less daunting and more realistic to execute.

Finally, a crucial part of self-motivation is decision making. This can be daunting, and it can pull strongly on your emotions. Making hard decisions is not always easy, and it can be damaging if not properly handled. There was an occasion when I had to release one of our vice presidents over company administration. This was difficult for me to do because he was close to several other leaders. Out of respect and fairness, I should have met personally with that individual before I allowed the chief operations officer to let him go, explaining why he was being released—but I didn't. He was rightfully angry that I didn't talk to him, and to this day, he is respectful but aloof toward me.

> A crucial part of self-motivation is decision making.

On another front, I oversaw a difficult decision to move our company's payday from every other Friday to every other Monday, knowing it would disturb many team members and possibly cause some to leave the company altogether. To achieve this transition without a major uprising, we decided to give everyone their first pay a week in advance and included extra compensation to cover the anticipated cost of the initial three-day delay. Most everyone saw it as a bonus and got on board with the change. It was a wonderful way to show that we had heard and understood their concerns and needs by giving them a way to plan ahead and adjust their personal expenditures such as paying bills or grocery shopping.

In the end, every decision you make has consequences—and your decisions today will determine your quality of life tomorrow. Your decisions sculpt your destiny.

With that in mind, *No Bad Days* will teach you how to develop and maintain the mindset required to make the right decisions so that every day matters.

We will explore the attributes of each day. What, exactly, make Sundays super?

We will examine the characteristics of each day. What are the common traits that make Mondays marvelous?

We will learn principles that define how Tuesdays are terrific, Wednesdays are wonderful, and so on.

By the time we're done, you'll never look at the calendar, your schedule—or your life—the same way again.

So, let's begin with what many people see as the first day of the week, even if it isn't the traditional start of the work week.

[1]

SUPER SUNDAY
Vision

Since its launch in 1920, the National Football League (NFL) had seen many potential rival leagues come and go, but when the American Football League (AFL) kicked off in 1960, it quickly began competing for fans and coveted television revenue.

Having a vision of being seen as legitimate and equal with the long-standing NFL, AFL commissioner Joe Foss sent an invitation to the NFL on January 14, 1961, to schedule a "World Playoff" game between the two leagues' champions beginning with the upcoming 1961 season. The game itself wouldn't happen for another six years, but when it did, the inaugural "AFL-NFL Championship Game" pitting the NFL champion Green Bay Packers against the AFL champion Kansas City Chiefs was an unexpected success.

By the time the third title game was played in January 1969, it was officially called the "Super Bowl," and when the AFL champion New York Jets upset the NFL's title holders, the Baltimore Colts, Joe Foss' original vision had come to pass.

Two seasons later, the two leagues merged to reform the NFL into the two conferences whose champions still face one another today—and the "Super Bowl," now one of the greatest annual sporting events in the world, continues to be played, quite fittingly, on a Sunday.

• • • • • • •

Discerning the beautiful

Anything super starts with a vision. I love its definition. Vision is an unusual competence in discernment of an extraordinarily beautiful thing which you see or experience in your mind. Please read that over again. Isn't it telling? There is no doubt that one of the greatest visions ever expressed to a country and its people was the one Dr. Martin Luther King Jr. discerned of a united America without judgment and racism. The following excerpt, from his speech on the steps of the Lincoln Memorial at The March on Washington for Jobs and Freedom on August 28, 1963, will remain among the most famous words ever spoken.

> Vision is an unusual competence in discernment of an extraordinarily beautiful thing.

"So even though we face the difficulties of today and tomorrow, I still have a dream. It is a dream deeply rooted in the American dream. I have a dream that one day this nation will rise up and live out the true meaning of its creed, 'We hold these truths to be self-evident, that all men are created equal.' ... I have a dream that my four little children will one day live in a nation where they will not be judged by the color of their skin but by the content of their character."[1]

Yet long before he made that great speech, Dr. King had implemented the Beloved Community, a group of people committed to, and trained in, the philosophy and methods of nonviolence. This was the cornerstone of the principles used by those involved in the civil rights movement of the 1950s-60s. They believed in a global vision where poverty, hunger, and homelessness were not to be tolerated because international standards of decency wouldn't allow it. In this vision, racism and all forms of discrimination and prejudice were to be replaced by an all-inclusive spirit of brotherhood and sisterhood.

Now that's a vision that communicates "an unusual competence in discernment of an extraordinarily beautiful thing." Dr. King saw and experienced this in his mind, and he dedicated his life—and ultimately lost it—doing everything he could to make it a reality.

As it was for Dr. King, so it can be for you. Your vision is *part* of who you are and what you are doing or are going to do. *Who* you are is your purpose, your reason for existing. Many times, people don't see their purpose, but when it is crafted into a vision, both they and others can see and experience it. No wonder pastor, author, and leadership expert Bill Hybels said, "Vision is a picture of the future that produces passion."

For example, let's say I declare a vision to travel around the world and speak. Then I get more specific, indicating that I want to go to Africa. I begin to talk about going to Africa and believing that things are going to open up for me to do so. That includes speaking with people and describing what I wish to see happen, detailing the countries or cities I wish to visit, what I want to achieve there, and what needs to be accomplished for me to get there. I talk about going to Africa in such a way that others are going to be able to see what I am saying—proclaiming my vision as purpose in picture form as though I was painting it onto a canvas. This results in providing people an opportunity to help fulfill the vision and make it come to pass.

As you begin discerning the beautiful to create purpose-driven visions that you want to achieve in your life, there are three truths about vision that will guide you in the process.

1. Vision will put you in over your head (beyond your human capacity), but never beyond your potential, to produce. When I first started my leadership consultant firm, Vision Excellence Company, I had a vision that I would be teaching before multimillion dollar organizations. That was very much outside of my immediate circles of influence and was over the top of what I had done in the past. But my vision kept me hungry, and that hunger encouraged me to keep studying, learning, and striving for excellence. Within five years, I found myself conducting an Emotional Intelligence seminar at a Christian ministry headquarters in Philadelphia, Pennsylvania—the national hub of a multimillion-dollar organization. My vision had been fulfilled. Since then, I've worked with no less than a dozen other companies that size, affirming my continuing potential to achieve the goal I envisioned.

2. Vision will be assaulted by criticism. In the early 2000's, I developed a vision to return to and build up the neighborhood where I was raised as a boy, Westgate in Decatur, Alabama. A low-income area, Westgate was characterized by its project housing and the shopping center featuring a Piggly Wiggly supermarket. Most of the shops and restaurants had moved out, and I desired to bring national brand stores to the old shopping center and build new houses in a rundown old apartment complex. I saw a better life with better amenities for the great people that lived in that neighborhood.

When I did a presentation 15 years ago to the local Rotary Club and to officials at City Hall, they were all on board—but when news of my plan got out to the community, it was instantly attacked and criticized. Some even accused me of simply trying to get rich off the project. I did not let that stop me, though, and while the full project did not come to fruition, we did build a few homes and have since inspired others to invest in the neighborhood.

It was very frustrating that the people complained so much and went against my vision. The city government considered it for two years before we accepted that our plans simply weren't going to come to pass. Today, a subdivision with several homes has been built, but the shopping center is still the same. In all, Westgate is a little better off, but there is still much potential there.

3. Vision will develop you. As I pursue my vision of helping leaders reach their potential by maximizing their core values, it has led me to grow in many areas as well. I have needed to go back to school to get various certificates and training. This vision has placed me at the table with very influential leaders, which has pushed me to improve my communication skills. I have had to increase my financial and business acumen in order to better understand my potential customers. I am driven to get up every day with an expectation to learn and develop.

·······

A super day for visioncasting

What are the three attributes that make Sunday the ideal day to dream, visualize, and set into motion the visions for your life? First, it operates in the *law of first*, setting the expectation for the week. Back when I worked for General Motors, I began setting aside time every Sunday afternoon to cast a vision for each upcoming week. I wrote down what projects I wanted to work on and defined the degree of accomplishment for each project and the results I wanted to see. I continue this routine today, and it keeps me in line and on track with my goals. It motivates me to set expectations that are higher than I believe I can accomplish.

I'm the type of person who is always striving beyond my original motivation. As speaker Les Brown is quoted to have said, "Shoot for the moon, and if you miss, you'll still be among the stars." I truly believe that the problem with most people's goals is that they set them just low enough to hit them. Even when I don't hit my goals, I have still accomplished way more than most people can even imagine.

Second, Sunday is a day of *personal inspiration*, a time we are compelled to go forward. Over 20 years ago, I was inspired to have an hour of self-reflection about my future. I do this every Sunday, usually in the early evening and either in my outdoor gazebo at home or on a motorcycle ride. I ask myself "why," "how," and "when" questions that invite me to dream of my potential accomplishment, entertain ideas, and explore the options presented to me.

> I ask myself "why," "how," and "when" questions that invite me to dream.

Finally, I use Sundays as a weekly opportunity to *establish an intentional tone* for the scope and sequence of the week ahead. I first began this practice when I was in North Carolina working at IBM (International Business Machines Corporation). I wrote down ways I wanted to have a positive attitude for the week, and then I looked at the scope of work as far as who I needed to communicate with and when to provide them the highest level of positive engagement and feedback. I even planned my business attire choices for the week depending on who I was going to meet and where.

I continue to do this today before bedtime every Sunday night. It's a great way to end the day by solidifying my mindset and setting myself at ease about the coming work week.

Some other great things about Sunday are the characteristics uniquely common to the day. For many, it is a day of worship and reflection where our spiritual natures are nourished and activated. By focusing, if only for a few hours, on the divine, our hearts and minds are quieted, positioning us to better hear and ponder new insights or ideas. There was a Sunday in August 2019 when I had the insight to start a new program to talk about leadership. I saw a vision of inviting leaders from different backgrounds to talk live on YouTube about various topics concerning personal growth and leadership. I was inspired to reach out to several guests, and we started the program called Lead and Achieve with Doc Rock. It currently goes live every second and fourth Thursday evening of each month on the Emmanuel The Connection YouTube channel.

Sunday is also generally considered to be a day of rest. It's the one day where many people set aside additional time with their families to relax and play. Some use Sundays as an opportunity for a special in-town getaway, to take day trips away from home to see and do new things, or to revisit previous positive experiences. All of these things allow us to redirect our thoughts away from the urgent matters of the rest of the week, enabling us to think more freely and with less distraction.

While taking a ride one Sunday evening on my motorcycle, I was inspired to begin speaking in a different way as a pastor, one that would focus more on personal growth for businessmen and women while still advancing the Kingdom of God. I wanted my sermons to apply to people's everyday lives while breaking away from the traditional approach of an introduction, three points, and a conclusion. I even began bringing people onstage while I taught to supplement what I was sharing. Most of the presentations I now use for corporate America come from those teachings. Since then, my effectiveness as a pastor and as a consultant has been enhanced and deepened.

Because Sunday is situated on the calendar as the starting point of each new week, it is the perfect day for visioncasting—for it is through vision that seven key choices are made that directly impact your life every day.

1. Vision chooses your future. Growing up, I had always thought about being a doctor in a hospital. I would read my mom's nursing books, and I took all the science classes I could in high school. One day, while I was contemplating how to get into and pay for medical school, I visited Dr. Kenneth Pitts in Huntsville about a medical career. He was my mother's colleague, so I knew he would be a great person to give me some good advice.

I told him what I was thinking about doing. "You may very well have the intellect," he replied, "but what is God's vision for you?" He went on to explain that he became a doctor because he felt God had called him to go into that field, and he told me to return to him for help only after I had prayed. I did so—and that was when I was given a vision of leading people to achieve their best.

2. Vision chooses your friends. When I put into motion my vision to be involved with a leadership organization in the northern Alabama region, it led me to becoming friends with the CEO of the organization. Since then, I have met many others who have become close friends and with whom I can share ideas and dreams. Those relationships have benefitted me immensely and have led to the birth of other visions to do good work.

3. Vision chooses your library. My desire to learn more about how people's minds and emotions operated in concert with one another encouraged me to start reading books about proper mindset and Emotional Intelligence. My library is now full of books on positive thinking and personal and professional discipline, and I read or listen to such content every day, even if it is only for 10 minutes at a time.

4. Vision chooses your priorities. In 1997, "The Sound and the Fury" boxing match between Evander Holyfield and Mike Tyson for the WBA Heavyweight Championship was the sports event of the year, and several of my friends were getting together to watch it. I really wanted to join them—but because I had a vision for achieving success as a leadership trainer, I had to forego the invitation in order to prepare for a training session. I may have missed the big bite Tyson took from Holyfield's ear that night, but I took a far bigger bite toward meeting my goal and executing my vision by keeping my priorities.

5. Vision chooses your use of time. There have been many other occasions where my time had to be dedicated to work in order to achieve specific goals. One of those was when I had to spend extra hours as an engineer completing a new project on behalf of Saginaw Steering, a division of my employer, General Motors. The project involved creating an automatic torque machine that served as a wrench that attached a tube to the steering gear. I had a vision to see it come to fruition on deadline and with excellence, and I put in the time necessary to achieve that goal.

6. Vision chooses your values. Values are your standards, your principles of behavior. While I was in college, I was at a party where several fellow students were getting drunk, and it looked to me like things were getting out of hand. People were getting rowdy and raucous. I certainly didn't view myself as being better than anyone else who was there, but my values directed me to leave the party. I didn't want to do anything to undermine my vision of achieving everything I could while in engineering school. I encouraged my friends to be safe before departing, and I have never regretted the decision to honor my values.

7. Vision chooses your attitude in life. Countless times, I have made the decision to keep and maintain a positive attitude, especially when under pressure. Ability Plus is an organization subject to an annual state audit regarding the services we provide. In 2021, we were cited in several areas, and the auditor went over all the improvements needed for our organization to be in full compliance. It felt like the world and everyone in it was against me and the company, but I told the auditors that the issues were my responsibility as CEO and that we would address them, knowing it's always best to be proactive rather than reactive.

I had a vision of us going from "good to great," and I challenged everyone using the book of the same name by Jim Collins. Changes were implemented in operations, policies and procedures, and overall work culture. As a result, the staff's mindset was elevated, we dug in, and we worked with a vision of being triumphant. The next audit confirmed a 100-percent improvement in all facets of the company.

* * * * * * *

Super Sunday principles to complete your vision

I am always inspired by the stories of others who have achieved greatness. Four stories in particular serve to exemplify my four key principles for completing your vision.

First, you must be willing to *pay the price* regardless of the obstacles in front of you. Helen Keller once said, "The only thing worse than being blind is having sight but no vision," and she certainly knew that to be true. Helen was only 19 months old when she lost both her sight and hearing in 1881. At the age of seven, Helen met her first teacher, Anne Sullivan, who would become her lifelong companion. Helen learned language, including reading and writing, and Sullivan's first lessons focused on spelling words on Helen's hand to teach her the names of objects around her. Helen also learned how to speak and how to understand other people's speech.

> You must be willing to *pay the price* regardless of the obstacles.

Never allowing her physical conditions to limit her, Helen had a vision to achieve greatness in service to others. After attending both specialist and mainstream schools, Helen attended Radcliffe College of Harvard University and became the first deaf and blind person to earn a bachelor's degree. Helen worked for the American Foundation for the Blind from 1924 until 1968, touring the United States and traveling to 35 countries around the globe as an advocate for those with vision loss.

Helen ended up writing 14 books and hundreds of speeches and essays, and she tirelessly campaigned for those with disabilities as well as for women's suffrage and labor rights. A supporter of the National Association for the Advancement of Colored People, Helen was also an original member of the American Civil Liberties Union. Helen not only had incredible vision, but she paid the price to see it come to pass. Her persistence, perseverance, and tenacity remain an enduring example today.

When I was a student at Kettering University (formerly the GMI Engineering & Management Institute), I was voted by my peers to be the president of the Black Unity Congress (BUC). As its leader, I paid the price to fulfill my vision to get others involved in the BUC who were not African American. I wanted the organization to be genuinely supported by the entire student body. Several BUC members had serious reservations about moving in that direction. "If we include whites, are we still about black unity?" "Are they going to take over?" "Are we still going to focus on issues that affect minorities, or are they going to try to address other issues?" My answer was that we were going to bring in others because the issues we addressed were not just about us as African American, but they affected everyone.

It took considerable time and effort to convince the BUC that my vision to no longer be a segregated organization was a good idea. Several whites joined, including my good friend, Andrew, who was president of the student body. Under my tenure, we got more involved in the student body, developed a mentorship program with area churches, and sat in on the school's President's Council for the first time. Our funding also quadrupled. It took courage, but we were all willing to pay the price for a better tomorrow.

Next, you must be strong enough to *overcome persecution*. Corrie Ten Boom once said, "I can see further than my eyes can look." It's impossible to imagine the vision she had to develop in order to see beyond her experiences as a survivor of the Holocaust. It couldn't have been easy for Corrie to accept what her Nazi captors had done to her, tormenting her at Ravensbrück and causing the death of her sister, Betsy.

Ten years after her release, Corrie ran into a woman who refused to look her in the eyes. Confused, she asked about the lady, and she was told the woman had been a nurse at a concentration camp. Corrie then recalled taking Betsy to the infirmary to see that very nurse. Betsy was dying, and the woman had been cruel and sharp-tongued. At that moment, Corrie's hatred returned with a vengeance. Her rage so boiled that she knew of only one thing to do—and that was to get a vision to live as a forgiving person.

"Forgive me," she cried out. "Forgive my hatred, oh, Lord. Teach me to love my enemies!"

Suddenly, Corrie felt her anger being displaced with a love she couldn't explain. The next day, Corrie called the hospital where the nurse worked and invited the woman to a meeting where she was speaking. That evening after her talk, Corrie sat down with the nurse and shared how she had come to love God despite the atrocities done to her and to her sister. Thanks to Corrie's words and forgiveness, the woman also decided to trust in God. For Corrie, overcoming the persecution she had faced was only possible by having a vision to forgive those who had harmed her.[2]

When I started church ministry as a pastor over 25 years ago, I wanted to do things differently than our existing, mostly older membership had been. In general, they were satisfied attending church, having worship service, and doing Bible studies, but they were not doing holistic outreach for the community outside the church walls or for the parishioners themselves. I began inviting people from all ethnic backgrounds and walks of life to join us. I developed a program of empowerment, pushing individuals to look at entrepreneurship and personal development opportunities to better their lives.

Yet many in the church didn't understand this, and they began to persecute me and those who supported me. They talked about our efforts in negative ways and didn't like how aggressive we were in our outreach to the community. It was foreign to them. Still, we knew what we were doing was right, and we kept moving forward. As a result, we developed outreaches that trained people to get jobs and be accepted into institutions of higher learning. We taught people how to have and handle house mortgages, and over 60 percent of our parishioners stopped renting and began owning their own homes. It was amazing.

Third, completing your vision requires you to have a *commitment to core values*. Nick Saban is one of the most successful college football coaches in recent history, leading his teams to multiple national titles at Louisiana State University and the University of Alabama. Saban said, "You've got to have a vision of, 'What kind of program do I want to have?' Then you've got to have a plan to implement it. Then you've got to set the example that you want, develop the principles and values that are important, and get people to buy into it."

As told in 2018 by ESPN senior writer Kevin Van Valkenburg in ESPN The Magazine's college football issue, Saban's Alabama Crimson Tide had just defeated the University of Texas 37-21 to win Alabama's first national title since 1992. Here is what quarterback Greg McElroy said Saban told the team in the locker room after that victory. "To you seniors, I just want to thank you for everything you did. Absolutely amazing, everything you put into this program. You didn't choose us as a coaching staff, but you bought in when we got here, and you've been rewarded. We're grateful to you for that contribution." Then he added, "For those of you coming back, that's not the way we play in the second half, and you know that. I'm proud of you, too, but we're going to get that stuff figured out when we get back together in a couple of weeks."

Even at the peak of triumph, Saban remained true to the core values his players had bought into, and he reiterated that vision, which focused on maintaining superior performance on the football field, to his returning athletes—most of whom would respond with more title-winning performances in the future.

There was a time when a company I led was riding high. It was part of our core values to care for our staff at all of our locations, and we definitely had a dedicated team of workers who believed in our mission and were willing to sacrifice so we could be our best. We received some extra funding that could have been used for other programs, but I decided instead to give it to every person in the company in the form of bonuses to assist in their everyday lives. I felt that if we helped them individually to maximize who they were, then collectively we would maximize who *we* were. People were encouraged as we stayed true to our core values. It showed them that they mattered to us and that we valued their service.

Finally, you must *develop patience* to complete your vision. The late, great leadership expert and minister Dr. Myles Munroe once said, "Vision is eternity positioned in time." He knew this truth from an early age. When he was 14, Munroe learned that a trusted teacher from the United Kingdom had referred to him as a "black monkey" and said that "black people cannot learn sophisticated things." Humiliated and upset, Munroe told his mother about the insults. In response, she got out her Bible and instructed him to read Ephesians 3:20, which said God could help him do "exceedingly abundantly above all that we ask or think."

That message changed Munroe's mindset as he understood that power did not reside in his teacher's racist words but rested within. Patiently, Munroe pursued his education, graduated at the top of his class, and went on to college to obtain no less than three bachelor's degrees, a master's degree, and five doctorates. As he did, he became a speaker whose words had an eternal impact on the lives of others. What became of the teacher who insulted him? Munroe eventually met him in person at a leadership conference—and the teacher, who asked Munroe to autograph two books Munroe had written, apologized for way he had viewed Munroe as a student. Munroe replied, "Don't you ever again underestimate a human," and they embraced.[3]

I was born to a 15-year-old mother who taught me that I could achieve anything I put my mind to as long as I had the patience to pursue it. When I turned 16, I drove around my mom's little wrecked Toyota while my peers were driving their own new or used cars that were in much better shape than mine. I wanted us to have a different car, among other things, yet I knew that if I worked hard in school and made good grades, I could produce something great for us in the future. I patiently studied with expectation and anticipation that there would come a day when I could afford to have and do things that were not available to me then. I developed a mindset of delayed gratification, a principle that creates time to build money, talent, or resources in order to obtain something. That patience has paid off with a successful career that has generated wealth and resources for me and my family.

· · · · · · ·

Starting each week with renewed vision acts as a preview of things to come, setting the stage for success and allowing you to go into your Monday with momentum. Why?

Vision brings positive change. Sure, he was just a blacksmith, but Will Turner was also an artisan at creating beautiful swords, and he developed a vision to become expert at wielding them. As he dueled against the renegade buccaneer, Captain Jack Sparrow, inside the smithy where his swords were displayed, Will boasted, "I practice three hours a day so that when I meet a pirate, I can kill him!"

If you've seen the motion picture *Pirates of the Caribbean: The Curse of the Black Pearl*, you'll remember that later, at the opportune moment, Will's training paid off as he teamed with Jack to fight off the Pearl's crew, end the curse, and rescue the governor's fair daughter.

Developing and rehearsing your vision will have a similarly life-changing impact on yourself and those around you. When it comes to vision, I've learned that 10 percent of people are Pioneers, meaning they are those who desire to put in the work and take the risks necessary to fulfill their vision. They are on the cutting edge in their field and see what has not yet been produced. The next group are Settlers and account for 70 percent of individuals. They are those who just settle for the status quo, going with the flow and preferring the norm when it comes to what they see and experience. They are capable of developing and rehearsing their vision, but they choose not to.

> Developing and rehearsing your vision will have a life-changing impact.

Finally, the remaining 20 percent of people are Antagonistic. They are those who are negative about visioncasting and tend to see all of the potholes in the road instead of the road itself. They don't put in the work to create a vision because they don't even see the vision in the first place. About 15 years ago, my church had a vision to move to a new location. A few of our people (Pioneers) were very excited and willing to do whatever was necessary to make the move a success. Most (Settlers) were fine with moving and had no complaints, but they were not going to go out of their way to help make it happen. Then there was the last group (Antagonists) who loved to find the speck in the milk. They were negative about most everything having to do with the move.

In a business setting, Settlers rely on others to build the company and achieve its vision. They don't rely on themselves. They look to leadership to do it all. They do their jobs, go home, and come in the next morning to do their job again. Sometimes the culture of a company pushes that mindset to the forefront because it doesn't get people involved in change. As leaders, then, knowing the Pioneers are on board, we focus on the Settlers. Our management and teaching efforts target them with the hope that some might come over and join the 10 percent.

Knowing that there will be confrontation with the Antagonists, leaders should treat them well, but not allow them to undermine the vision. "Okay," we tell them, "you have your opinion. You see a different way, and that's fine." Yet leaders are to listen to the 20 percent and not alienate them. While they may come across as negative and critical, there could still be legitimacy in some of the things they say. We can learn from them to make the process better.

Vision fosters innovation and creativity, empowering you beyond your existing assets. Jupiter is a massive planet buffeted by immense storms. Scientists speculate these gigantic tempests, swirling with 400 mile-per-hour winds, have been raging unabated for hundreds of years. But it wasn't until recently that they learned the source of Jupiter's ultra-potent storms. The Galileo space probe revealed that they're generated not by sunlight, as are storms on Earth, but by the planet itself. Jupiter's storms actually churn 10,000 miles into the planet and are powered by its sizzling hot core.

Everything viewed on the surface of Jupiter starts at the very heart of the planet—and anything new and inventive in your life that's going to rise to the surface begins with the vision churning within you at your core, providing you the ability to see what others cannot.

When I was a young engineer working for Delphi, a division of General Motors, a vision was brewing within me to make a specific process (torquing a nut onto a tube) more efficient and reliable. It had been done the same way for years using a manual torque wrench gauge. The gauge was employed at the end of a process that had five stations. That meant that by the time the tube got to the inspection station, there was a chance that as many as five of the nuts were not properly torqued. My vision would electronically check each individual torque station and stop the line when there was an error. This required new electronic torque guns (the tools that tighten the nuts) as well as the updated process arrangement.

We called a team meeting to talk about the current process and how it functioned. I then shared how I saw the new process working. Instead of having a person on the end of the line that checked all the parts after they were torqued, I proposed that each person would have a gun to check the particular nut they were working on at their station. Whenever a bad torque happened, everybody had to be patient and wait for that person to retorque it. We also had to ensure that, whenever a bad part was detected, there was a person in charge of getting the replacement part and putting it in the proper bin. It took three months from start to finish, but we implemented my vision, and it increased both productivity and quality.

Why didn't others see what I did? Most people kept their head down, concerned only about the process instead of saying, "This is good, but how can it be better?"

I always say, "Good, better, best. Never let it rest until your good is better and your better is best." A good thing can be a bad thing if it's not the best thing, yet most people settle for good.

Vision causes simplicity. Clergyman Robert Fulghum became famous because of his essay, "All I Really Need to Know I Learned in Kindergarten." He suggested that the simple rules learned in kindergarten will do for life. Share everything. Play fair. Don't hit people. Put things back where you found them. Clean up your own mess. Flush.

Simplicity eliminates complication, bringing clarity of purpose and providing direction. There was a process change that I felt would make things work much smoother with our internal structure at Ability Plus. The vision was to streamline the roles of our Qualified Intellectual Disabled Professional (QIDP) staff into two different categories: office-specific and field-specific. As it was, our QIDP's were responsible for all the paperwork, including the processing forms required by the state, along with any issues that happened in the field in the house or with our clients. With the new process, half of them would be responsible for office work and the other half for field duties. That would allow each QIDP to operate within their strengths and work together to get the job done, bringing greater value to the entire team. The new vision's strength was how it brought a sense of order and created simplicity.

Violins made by masters like Antonio Stradivari produce an incomparably beautiful sound and sell for millions to investors. But excellent violins are not like works of art, to be hung on a wall or displayed under glass. They'll lose their tone if not played regularly, and they actually increase in value the more they're used. That's why the Stradivari Society exists. It puts those first-rate violins into the hands of great violin virtuosos to ensure the instruments are preserved, cared for, and played. The musicians are even required to give the violin owners two command performances each year.

You possess a prized possession more valuable than any worldly investment: your attitude. As you change your mindset, you will become a virtuoso at whatever you do—and there's no better day than Monday to establish your attitude for the week.

[2]

MARVELOUS MONDAY
Attitude

Both the hummingbird and the vulture fly over our nation's deserts. All vultures see is rotting meat because that is what they are looking for. They thrive on that diet. But hummingbirds ignore the smelly flesh of dead animals. Instead, they look for the colorful blossoms of desert plants. They fill themselves with freshness and life. Vultures live on what was. They feed on the past. Hummingbirds live on what is. They seek new life from the present.

That insightful story, as told by writer Steve Goodier in Reader's Digest's Quote Magazine, illustrates a tremendous truth about attitude. We feed upon and become what we see—not with our eyes, but with our minds. There is nothing as powerful as your mindset, and as I often say, "You are today what you thought yesterday, and you will be tomorrow what you are thinking today."

Mondays become marvelous when we start each workweek with the right mindset, and mindset begins and ends with attitude. Prior to this book, I wrote and published *God-A-Tude*, which focuses on developing an attitude that brings success to life, and I mentioned how surprised I was that many people are simply not aware of how their attitude plays such a major part in their success. Yet more opportunities have been lost, withheld, or forfeited because of attitude than from any other cause.

Yet attitude is our way of thinking. It is the mindset, or mental conditioning, that determines our interpretation of, and response to, our environments. Your attitude dictates how you react to the present, and it determines the quality of your future. It creates your world and designs your destiny. You are your attitude, and your attitude is you. If you do not control your attitude, it will control you.

> You are your attitude, and your attitude is you.

• • • • • • •

Having a "champion" mindset

Monday is marvelous because it possesses four distinct attributes that allow you to win!

1. Monday positions you to be humble. The first day of the workweek can appear awfully daunting, even after you've done everything you can on Sunday to ready yourself for the week ahead. Therefore, you can respond in one of two ways. You can pridefully rush forward into it, or you can humbly step back a moment, assess it, and then move onward in calm confidence. Humility is both a bedrock trait and a powerful asset in your "champion" mindset. The definition of "humble" is telling: "showing a modest estimate of one's own importance." Isn't that remarkable?

The way up is down. You have to get down before you can go up!

From the time I was 17 until my mid-thirties, I felt like I was better than other people. I knew I had been gifted to achieve, and in those 18 years I had experienced success. There I was, this guy from government housing who was traveling around the world teaching leadership principles for life. I had become a little full of myself, lacking in proper humility. Then, in 2008, the economy tanked, and organizations began to struggle. My support system started to crumble. Many who had been contributing to my travel expenses stopped supporting me. Organizations were not asking me to come as frequently as they once did. Just like that, I came back to earth, and as I examined what was going on, I realized I had become arrogant in my outlook.

That caused me to take a long look at *myself*. Today, I refer to this introspection as a checkup from the neck up and a look around from the shoulders down. I asked, "Am I doing what I am doing for fame or to impress people, or am I doing it to help people?" It was a great question. I came to the conclusion that I wanted to help others—but to do that, I had to remove all of the self-serving perks that came from people saying I'd done a good job or patting me on the back. Receiving accolades is fine as long as you keep it in proper perspective. In all, it took several months for me to change my attitude so that I wasn't going in thinking people needed to treat me as some prima donna, but as a servant. "Can I help them?" "Are they receptive?" "Can I maximize their potential?" It had to stop being about me, and it had to start being about them.

Walking in a position of humility requires you to accept that you have weaknesses. Everyone does, but many will not acknowledge them, which in the end, generally leads to times of struggle. I often tell others that they will grow when they exalt their strengths and work on their weaknesses. In my case, my weaknesses were arrogance and impatience. The strengths I exalted were that I engaged people, made them feel good, and could show individuals and organizations a vision so they could proceed.

To be humble, you must also be open to correction and the opportunity to learn from others who are ahead of you. Mentorship and coaching are the best ways to do this. Working with a mentor is crucial, and coaching takes that another step, allowing you to systematically put into practice what you learn with your mentor. Simply put, when you take the time and dedicate the money to invest in yourself, it is always going to pay dividends greater than you can anticipate.

2. Monday encourages you to have self-control. Monday is the one day of the week when you don't want things to get away from you. Otherwise, you can't help but feel like you're always having to play catch up. So, while there will be situations that you cannot control, you can control yourself—what you think, how you operate, and the way you respond to the circumstances that come your way. To be someone who exhibits an ability to control your emotions and moderate your words and actions, you cannot allow a flash of negative emotions to produce negative results.

Self-control is all about holding it together when your world seems to be falling apart.

I remember a time as a chief operating officer when my chief executive officer treated me like I was a nobody without any respect. He made demands on my time without asking me if I had the time available. It was always his way or no way. At one point, I felt like I was an angry kid back in the projects, and I wanted to knock him out!

Yet I knew that my future had promise, and I told myself that it was not worth it to respond that way. I also decided that my philosophy of being a servant leader would eventually rise to the top and show others who I really was. I exercised self-control by telling myself that the company and the people who worked for me were more important than my desire to prove a point or do something that I would regret. I thought about them and how I wanted them to look at leadership, knowing they looked up to me. I consulted with mentors outside of the company, and I was able to continue dealing with the situation until he was released as the CEO. I then used the Emotional Intelligence disciplines of self-awareness and self-management to keep my goals and projects headed in the right direction.

The process of working on your self-control involves looking ahead at your desired future. So many people lose their way because they have not learned to accept temporary pain to get to long-term joy. When you have a true vision of where you are going and what you want to be, it encourages you to gather yourself when you want to fly off the handle. When you realize how much there is to lose, you better appreciate having the self-control to keep what you have gained.

3. Monday inspires you to have a willingness to learn. On Monday, there is almost always something new or unexpected that beckons or forces you to acquire knowledge you didn't have before or to recall something you previously learned and apply it. To gather ideas from a variety of sources, accurately evaluate the situation, and combine good ideas with the details of the circumstance in order to make changes in your behavior, personally or organizationally, is an essential component of maintaining a "champion" mindset.

You must use information to address your situation.

I was originally educated as an engineer: learning formulas, equations, and science in general. Then I was given the opportunity to learn, as a coach and consultant, how to help people reach their dreams and goals in life. Executive and leadership coaching required a new set of skills to move on to what I needed to know to succeed.

I embraced the new material as a student of change and a pupil of understanding. During my training program, I went through actual scenarios of how to talk to people and the questions to ask them as a coach. I did role playing. I read books on becoming a better listener. After an intense three months of learning, I was released to do some executive coaching, in part because of my previous background of being a church pastor and administrator. I continued training once a week for another year before I was fully let go. It was a full year from the time I began my training before I launched the Vision Excellence Company.

You will inspire yourself to learn when you see a benefit that is greater than the sacrifice of the learning process. When I first started training, I saw what other coaches and consultants were doing for organizations, and I thought becoming a coach and consultant would benefit me and the companies that hired me. Learning is the necessary seed to plant in order to gain the greater harvest you are looking for in your life. Learners are achievers!

4. Monday compels you to have a drive for more. When you've done the vision casting and preparation I recommend on Sunday, you can't help but go into Monday excited and optimistic, and that breeds M.O.R.E. (Multiple Opportunities Regardless of Everything against you). In every aspect of your life and career, there are greater heights to be experienced, greater accomplishments to achieve, greater impact to be had, greater knowledge to be obtained, greater wisdom to be acquired, greater good to be done—and, yes, more customers to acquire, more markets to penetrate, more employees to hire, more revenue to realize, and more influence to extend.

You are to go more, do more, and be more than you ever thought before!

"I want more!" That was what I told myself in 2018 when things were going well with Vision Excellence Company. I appreciated the opportunities to teach leadership in non-profit settings, but I knew I had more to give to for-profit companies and organizations. I had loved, and still love, teaching church leaders, but I wanted to expand. That required more study and additional branding to broaden my influence.

> You are to go more, do more, and be more than you ever thought before!

That's when I created "Doc Rock." The brand is more than just a simple play on my credentials and my name. "Doc Rock" literally communicates expertise and stability, and it suggests engagement, servanthood, and leadership. That new brand, and the services I provide through it, such as my twice-weekly video sessions via YouTube, have led me to go into many areas of motivational speaking and all types of leadership and business trainings that were previously unavailable to me.

To push yourself for more, you must ask yourself, "Is where I am now *all* that I want to do?" More requires greater sacrifice, and your "why" must be solid and defined early on, for challenges will come that will tempt you to stop at a place of comfort. Consider this: "If you had all the money in the world, what would you do?" The answer to that question will drive you to the core of who you are—the core that will take you to more!

* * * * * * *

Monday is also marvelous because of its three identifying characteristics that build and support your "champion" mindset.

1. Monday is a day that promotes work ethic. If there is ever a "nose to the grindstone" day in the week, it is Monday. You want to dig in and get things off to a productive start. This requires constantly looking for ways to do things more effectively and efficiently. Such diligence is often what propels already-successful people to start their own businesses and strive for even more greatness.

Work ethic is that something extra that gets you out of bed when others are still hitting the snooze button.

The trainer of the late, great professional basketball superstar, Kobe Bryant, got the call while he was still asleep, and who could blame him? It was 3:30 a.m. when his phone rang. Kobe told him that he was doing some conditioning work and could use his help. The trainer arrived at the gym an hour later to find Bryant practicing by himself. Drenched in sweat, the trainer thought it looked like Kobe had just jumped in a swimming pool. But the trainer wasn't at all surprised: he knew Bryant always put in the extra time and effort required to be exceptional.[4]

In 1992, I was fresh out of college and working for IBM as a young engineer. Another team member and I were given a project that required more time than usual to complete. It involved taking an existing printed circuit board and repurposing it for a better use. This necessitated getting to the office early for several weeks and included many late evenings staying at work and testing the new process. Our strong shared work ethic caused us to have great success with the project, and it paid off (literally) with both of us receiving a nice monetary award.

To create and maintain your work ethic, you must major on what is important and set proper priorities. Work ethic is all about performing at the highest level to achieve the highest result!

2. Monday is a day that requires the courage of a lion. Isn't it uncanny how often the adage of Murphy's Law—anything that can go wrong will go wrong—comes to pass on a Monday? There's no telling why this is, but I know I've faced my share of difficulties at the start of the workweek. These trials have usually extended themselves into the rest of the week, and they have necessitated courage to see them through. Courage is the choice and willingness to confront uncertainty, intimidation, danger, and even agony. Physical courage can manifest itself as a result of enduring pain and hardship. Moral courage can show itself in the face of opposition, shame, scandal, discouragement, or personal loss.

Courage is being scared to death but going forward anyway.

Remember the character of the Cowardly Lion from The Wizard of Oz? He was all growl but no bite, lacking vim or verve. He boasted, "I'll fight you with one paw tied behind my back," yet sobbed miserably when Dorothy slapped him for chasing Toto. "You're nothing but a great big coward!" she said as the so-called King of the Forest wiped away tears with his tail. Why, he couldn't even count sheep to fall asleep because he was afraid of them.

When I was asked to become the CEO of Ability Plus years ago, I could have been quite cowardly. The company was in a very bad financial position. The culture within the organization was toxic at best, and there was no strategic plan or outlook for the near future. I knew I had the leadership skills within me to build a team that could turn it around—but the fear that I might fail required me to summon courage like I never had before. Of course, I could have simply walked away and went somewhere else, but I saw a bright future for the organization beyond what my eyes were seeing and my emotions were feeling.

So, with knees shaking and heart pounding, much like the Cowardly Lion when he first faced the Wizard of Oz, I went before the entire company employee team and said, "We can do it! We can be one of the best in the industry!" I attacked my fear with courage and exhorted the other leadership and staff at Ability Plus to do the same. In less than a year, the company was on sure footing and would ultimately set the standard for serving people with intellectual disabilities.

To courageously confront whatever obstacles come against you on Monday, or any day, develop a mindset that you will either win or learn, but you cannot lose! Do not be afraid of failure. In fact, see failure as what it is: a part of the winning equation.

3. Monday is a day that necessitates synergy. On a day where unexpected challenges or stress can sometimes spur argument and division, the ability to have synergy is vital. I love the definition of synergy. Read it carefully. It is "an interaction or cooperation giving rise to a whole that is greater than the simple sum of its parts." Wow! The term "synergy" comes from the Greek word *synergia* and means "working together."

Over the years, I've discovered that most people compete in life—either with others at their own level, or, if they are seeking rapid growth, with those who are far more advanced than them.

Yet a better approach is to avoid competition and, instead, collaborate with others who are ahead of you.

For example, surveys have shown that most people prefer to go to a gym and work out alone. However, those who have experienced the benefits of pushing themselves physically with a trainer find the idea of working out alone downright comical. In other words, if you want to get stronger or faster, exercise with people who are in far better shape than you.

Likewise, if you want to do incredible work, partner with people who are more talented than you. One of the richest Americans of all time, industrialist and philanthropist Andrew Carnegie, said that teamwork appeared most effective when each individual helped others to succeed. The synergy of that team increased as each person contributed. The different skills of each team member also improved, which increased the efficiency of the team and developed its unity.

In everything you do, there should be collaborative and synergistic elements in play.

One of the best trainings I ever did was when my friend, Jeff Bright, and I collaborated on a presentation about Emotional Intelligence. Our synergy was amazing. We are very different in many ways, but those differences allowed us to pull on each other from all directions and to communicate to our audience in a much broader and deeper way. He was better than me in some areas; I was better than him in others. But together we taught about Emotional Intelligence in a way that was truly "greater than the simple sum of its parts." We received many positive comments on the effectiveness of our training.

In order to achieve synergy when divisive challenges arise, you must be open to new ideas and new ways of doing things. You should also be humble enough to accept that someone may have a better process than you that will make *you* better as you work together. Don't compete. Collaborate!

....

Monday mental strength

The Chicago Tribune once told of an interesting study where one group of volunteers was given a report stating that the "Monday blues" are real. The second was provided an article refuting its existence. A final group was given nothing at all. Guess what happened? The first group was most likely to rate Monday as the worst day of the week.[5]

If you firmly believe that Monday is always going to be a difficult day, odds are good it will be, but only because your attitude is dictating your outlook. A "champion" mindset requires you to be mentally strong—and your Monday will always be marvelous when you define the day by living out these 10 principles of mentally strong people.

> A "champion" mindset requires you to be mentally strong.

Fight through hurt and pain

A reporter once asked boxing legend, Muhammad Ali, how many sit-ups he did every day. "I don't count my sit-ups," Ali said. "I only start counting when it starts hurting, when I feel pain, 'cause that's when it really matters." You always have two choices when things begin to get tough: you can either overcome an obstacle and grow in the process, or you can let it beat you. If you quit when things get difficult, it'll be that much easier to quit the next time. On the other hand, if you force yourself to push through a challenge, your mental strength increases.

Years ago, while I was serving as a senior leader in church ministry, a person who was dear to the organization decide to leave. This particular individual had several key roles of responsibility, was close to my family, and was someone I trusted. If I could have carved out an executive assistant position for her, I would've done it 100 times over. I asked her to stay, but I realized it was selfish to want something for me when the departure would be better for her. I had to process that there would be pain, hurt, and disappointment as we grew and moved forward. In the end, the move was best for her, and going through it made me stronger as a leader.

Be patient and delay gratification

A famous experiment at Stanford University involved an administrator leaving a child alone in a room for 15 minutes with a marshmallow. Before leaving, the administrator told the child that she was welcome to eat it, but if she waited until he returned, she would get a second marshmallow. The children who were able to wait experienced better outcomes later in life, including higher college entrance exam scores, greater career success, and even lower body mass indexes.

The delay of gratification and patience are essential to success and mental strength. I once wanted everything right now—but that all changed when I had to wait for opportunities to be a keynote speaker and facilitator of seminars at major company events. I had the work ethic and the talent to do it immediately, and I wanted to experience the feeling of being valued as I walked out onto the big stage. I could see the lights and hear my name being announced. The atmosphere of success screamed at me, but I had to train my mind to endure every aspect of the hard work, critique, challenges, and pain necessary to see that manifested. During this time of delayed gratification, I learned that my ego was getting in the way. I had to stop making it about me and instead become humble and selfless, making it about others. It required a mindset shift where, instead of seeing what being a keynote speaker and facilitator would do for me and my success, I needed to focus on the value I would add to those I would serve. Going through that process gave me the right perspective and attitude when that level of success finally arrived.

Fail, make mistakes, and try again—without flinching

In a study at the College of William and Mary, researchers interviewed over 800 entrepreneurs and found that the most successful among them tended to have two critical things in common: they were terrible at imagining failure, and they did not to care what other people thought of them. In other words, they put no time or energy into stressing about their failures because they viewed failure as a small, but necessary, step in the process of reaching their goals.

When I was a young church pastor, we had a vibrant, growing ministry. But there came a time when the wheels fell off after I changed how I shared my sermons and presented my ministry to target a broader audience. We lost our members, revenue, and building. I fully believed in what I was doing, but I felt like a failure at first. I was embarrassed, too, and it was as if I had slipped into a deep, dark hole with no help or light in sight. My mind told me to stop, but my heart said to go forward and keep moving ahead despite negative comments or concerns. I couldn't predicate my feelings and choices on a bunch of other people, and I began to instead view my perceived failure as a part of success. I got to the point where I didn't care what people thought. I only cared about what I was called to do. I didn't flinch, and over time, the ministry recovered, and its impact expanded.

Keep your emotions and feelings in check

Negative emotions challenge your mental strength. While it's impossible not to feel your emotions, it is completely within your power to manage them effectively and to keep yourself in control of them. A bad mood can make you lash out or stray from your chosen direction just as easily as a good mood can make you overconfident and impulsive. There was a time that I got very angry when a person falsely accused me of a wrongdoing. That individual sent targeted emails to specific people that painted me in a bad light. I wanted to lash out, but I knew that was not the right thing to do. I kept my emotions in check, maintained the right perspective, and it worked out for my good. The truth came out, I was exonerated, and the company came out in a favorable light.

Make the calls you're afraid to make

Sometimes you have to do things you don't want to do because you know they're for the best. It's easy to let such challenges paralyze you, but mentally strong people know that, in these moments, the best thing they can do is to get started right away. Every moment spent dreading the task subtracts time and energy from actually getting it done. At Ability Plus, there was a time when I had to make a call to keep or drop a critical service at the company. There was no doubt that the service was needed in the community, but we simply did not have the proper resources and company buy-in to achieve excellence and success with that service. After much internal debate, I cancelled the service. Thankfully, we were able to find assistance to help relocate the service with another organization.

Trust your gut

There's a fine line between doing this well and being impulsive. Trusting your gut is a matter of looking at a decision from every possible angle. Then, when the facts don't present a clear alternative, believe in your ability to make the right decision. I had to follow my gut when I was presented with a plan for restructuring at Ability Plus. We streamlined the roles of our Qualified Intellectual Disabled Professional (QIDP) staff into two different categories: office-specific and field-specific. It had never been done that way before, and it was unnerving for some. Yet I'm so glad I went with my gut and made half of them responsible for office work and the other half for field duties. We may not have made it through the COVID-19 pandemic intact, when it hit in early 2020, had we not had the new structure.

Lead when no one else follows

It's not hard to set a direction and to believe in yourself when you have support, but the true test of mental strength is how well you maintain your resolve when nobody else believes in what you are doing. Stay the course as you try to win people over to your way of thinking. After all, a true vision is worth pursuing, even when you have to go it alone.

When I first started my quest to do paid leadership training seminars and events, there were many people who did not believe I would succeed. It may have seemed they were right when some of my early seminars went largely unattended except for the few individuals I had hired to work the event. But I just kept preparing material, leading, and believing until people started to show up. When no one was there, I still taught the seminar. It was great practice, and it solidified the material in my mind.

Focus on the details even when it makes your mind numb

Nothing tests your mental strength like mind-numbing details, especially when you're tired. Yet the more you are challenged, the more you should dig in and welcome it. When I started my senior year thesis project for my engineering degree and realized the details that I had to provide to get my thesis approved, my brain started to hurt. I was tasked with solving a major breakage problem with a radiator tank made of 33 percent glass-filled nylon. It took a year of researching the operations of three separate plants and massive analysis before I solved the problem and turned in my thesis. It ended up getting an award, and the solution I discovered is now openly available to other engineers to study and implement.

Be kind to people who are impolite to you

When people treat you poorly, it is tempting to stoop to their level and return the favor. When you have mental strength, you don't allow others to walk all over you, but you also do not have to be rude to them. Instead, treat impolite and cruel people with the same kindness you extend to everyone else. Don't allow their negativity to bring you down.

When I was in engineering school, one of my professors was very rude to me in front of my classmates because of my accent. I had not experienced anything like that from other educators, and it was quite embarrassing. His open criticism made me feel inadequate and brought on frustration. I never came back at him with any disrespect, but I kept a positive attitude, determined to perform at a high level in his class. I knew I had to do so in order to graduate, and I didn't want his negativity to delay me from reaching that goal.

Be accountable for your actions, no matter what
People are far more likely to remember how you dealt with a problem than they are to recall how it was created in the first place. So, instead of making an excuse, hold yourself accountable. That will show that you care about results more than your ego. One evening when I was under a lot of pressure and very stressed out, my teenage daughter asked me a question about an event. I responded to her in a rude way, and it didn't set well with her. I could see that I had offended her. I knew I had to be accountable for my actions, so I told her that I was sorry for my response and asked for her forgiveness. She granted it, the situation was resolved, and we were able to reengage right away.

••••••••

To take an attitude that creates a "champion" mindset and *use it* to bring success to your life, you need something to fuel that process and propel you forward.

That fuel is belief—and there's nothing like it to make your Tuesday's turn out terrific every time.

[3]

TERRIFIC TUESDAY
Belief

The Little Engine That Could by Watty Piper is a children's tale about a happy train loaded with food and toys. On the way to its destination, the train breaks down and becomes worried about all the kids who will not be able to play with the toys and eat all the yummies. Three different trains come by, but each one refuses to help because they are too proud, self-important, or tired.

Finally, a blue train shows up, and the toys desperately explain their situation and beg for help. The little engine thinks about all the good little boys and girls on the other side of the mountain who will not have any toys or food unless she helps. Despite its small size, the blue engine repeats the mantra, "I think I can, I think I can" over and over again as it pulls the train over the mountain. When it arrives, The Little Blue Engine repeats, "I thought I could. I thought I could."

The story's timeless lesson is simple and enduring: we can accomplish great things when we believe—and there's no better way to follow up your Marvelous Monday attitude than with a Terrific Tuesday of confident belief!

As the second day in the workweek, Tuesday is unique because it's the day that you want to create the **momentum** you need to carry you through the rest of the week. Ideally, Monday saw you getting off to a strong start. Your mindset is balanced and positive. Then Tuesday arrives with its sense of, "Okay, now how can I build upon that and keep this going?" That's where momentum comes in.

Simply defined, momentum is the impetus gained by a moving object. Scientifically stated, the momentum of an object is given by the product of its mass and the velocity. For example, a baseball is heavier than a tennis ball. If both the balls are thrown with the same velocity, more force is required to stop the baseball. Therefore, the force is directly proportional to the *mass* when the speed is constant. If two baseballs are thrown with different velocities, even more force is required to stop the ball with the higher pace. Therefore, the force is directly proportional to the *speed* at a constant mass.

Now, don't worry, there won't be a pop quiz on this at the end of the chapter, but how does this apply to you? Think about it. When you acquire and maintain momentum, you will arrive at your desired destination in a timely manner no matter how fast or slow others are moving around you. Likewise, you will have so much momentum that it would take something rather substantial to slow you down, much less stop you.

Momentum gets you where you need to go quickly and with pace. We need that on a Tuesday, don't we? Plus, momentum facilitates your belief and helps you to fulfill it. As The Little Blue Engine repetitively told itself, "I think I can, I think I can," it created momentum. In the end, there was no mountain high enough to prevent it from making its delivery.

There are five attributes that will make your Tuesday both terrific and momentum filled—and they stem from **belief combined with action**. What you *do* will compel your belief forward and make it a reality! What does this require?

1. Being steadfast. Steadfastness means being resolutely or dutifully firm and unwavering. It speaks to having faithfulness and loyalty.

I had to stay firm when I was attending GMI Engineering & Management Institute and was tempted to switch colleges. A bit homesick and overwhelmed with classwork, I thought it would be nice to be closer to home at Georgia Tech University. But I had been accepted at GMI with the help of some great people, not the least of whom was my mentor, Dr. David Green Jr. I decided to talk to him, and he was convinced I could do the work and handle all of the challenges at GMI. "Karockas," he said, "I brought you up here because I saw your work ethic and saw you overcome some things in your life, so I know you can do it. It is *in* you." With his exhortation, I chose to be loyal to him and faithful to what he declared was inside of me. I stayed steadfast to my commitment and in my work ethic. Three years after that meeting with Dr. Green, I graduated from GMI with a mechanical engineering degree. I also received the outstanding thesis award mentioned in the previous chapter.

When you are steadfast, the self-belief that emerges is **self-efficacy**. An intense level of self-efficacy is supported by your steadfastness as you get a chance to witness your skills and talents in action. You see what you can do, and that removes doubt. It shows you that you are likely better than you thought, and that you can do more. Still, even as Dr. Green told me what he saw in me, I nevertheless had to go do it. Once I witnessed my achievements, it made me confident, and my self-efficacy blossomed.

2. Being immovable. To be immovable is to remain fixed or unchangeable. It speaks to not yielding, whatever the obstacle.

Starting around 2018, I observed a disturbing nationwide trend. It seemed as though many leaders were thinking about their own success without any regard to those who were following them. It was about getting all they could at the expense of others.

But I had always believed in and taught servant leadership. So, I decided to stand firm in serving others ahead of myself. I placed my staff and their concerns before mine. It was not always easy to do. I had personally witnessed some self-centered leaders who made temporary gains in finances, position, and praise, and I could've become just as selfish. I could have acquired more things, made more money, and moved in greater circles of influence. Those temptations were there. Yet I knew that my leadership style was the right thing to do. The result? Those under my leadership at two different organizations grew and found fulfillment in their various areas of work and expertise.

When you are immovable, the self-belief that emerges is **self-control.** You become stationary in who you are and have control over the outside influences and forces that are trying to move you in the wrong direction. Self-control allows you to identify and understand your parameters. It keeps you steady, not swaying from one place to the next. Like a competitive swimmer, you stay in your own lane to win your race regardless of what everyone else is doing. A noted neuroscientist recently said, "There is no traffic when you are in your own lane." That's so true! You know when to kick it in. You know when to slow it down. Self-control allows you to have the discipline you need to stay on course and succeed.

3. Being always abounding. Abounding means to exist in large numbers or amounts. It speaks to being constantly plentiful to the benefit of yourself and others.

Sometimes we need to abound to justify what we desire and achieve it. In Chapter 1, I shared about the time I was president of the Black Unity Congress in college and needed to secure extra funding for our plentiful work of supporting minority students in school and in civic life. Yet the school was less than five percent African American, so to get the money, we had to drive up membership. That meant becoming more inclusive to the entire student body and no longer remaining a segregated organization.

We upped our recruitment efforts, regularly setting up a table in the lunchroom. We did everything we could to find students who had a heart for what we stood for and wanted to help. What happened? We more than doubled our membership, including the addition of the student body president. A white man, his involvement sent a clear message that the Black Unity Congress was for everybody. We ended up having one of the highest budgets of any student government organization on campus.

When you are always abounding, the self-belief that emerges is **self-assurance.** That gives you the attitude that whatever it is that you want *will* happen. You actively look for a positive result. Being always abounding feeds your mindset.

4. Knowing that your efforts are not in vain. If something is in vain, that means it was useless because it did not achieve anything. So, this speaks to being confident that what you are doing is useful and will achieve great things.

All of us wonder at times if what we are doing is useful or just wasting time. Back in 1998, my church, Emmanuel: The Connection Church, launched a separate, non-profit organization called Victory Hope to help at-risk kids. Three days a week, we would pick up about 20 kids after school and bring them to our facility to tutor them, give life skills training, and essentially love on them. Each visit included a full, nutritious meal.

Yet there were many occasions when the students, ranging from first graders all the way to high school seniors, got angry with us and demonstrated actions of ungratefulness. They stomped around or called us names. We understood that their behavior largely stemmed from their home life and away-from-home environments. Whatever was put into them came out. It was a lot of work for our crew of eight adults, and we sometimes questioned if we really were making a difference. But we were! Several of the kids who came through Victory Hope went on to do great things in life and fulfill their goals and dreams. Many got college degrees and worked good jobs. Others started businesses.

When you know that your efforts are not in vain, the self-belief that emerges is **self-confidence.** When you know that you are achieving something and that someone is or will benefit from your actions, it gives you confidence in your ability to facilitate change and the determination to keep going.

5. Fulfilling your actions as a labor of love. A labor of love is a task done for pleasure, not reward. Wow! Isn't that profound? This speaks to selflessly enjoying your work.

I have often said that love is a verb. It is an action, not a noun. When the COVID-19 pandemic first broke out, many people in our community in northern Alabama suffered from a lack of food. They were from all races and all ages, all demographics and all socioeconomic backgrounds, and I had never seen anything like it before. When I saw them standing in line for hours hoping to receive food and household supplies from a Christian ministry in Huntsville, it broke my heart and moved me to action. Ability Plus and Emmanuel: The Connection Church partnered to give out food boxes one Saturday morning. In all, we gave away a couple thousand boxes of non-perishable food: nuts, rice, cereal, and beans. It was hard, but incredibly rewarding, work. As we demonstrated love and cared for others, many people were blessed.

When you fulfill your actions as a labor of love, the self-belief that emerges is **self-esteem**. You cannot help but feel good about how you are impacting the situation and feel great about yourself for being involved in the work. Giving of yourself always elevates your self-esteem.

Every Tuesday, I compel my self-belief forward by doing *one thing* to brighten someone's day and intentionally do a kind act for them. At work, I might help one of our managers by taking a box they need to their office or bringing them a cup of coffee. I may help someone at the store by paying for their groceries. Whatever it is, I am not looking to get anything back—and it does wonders for my self-esteem. When I help someone else, I feel better about myself. Doing that one thing every Tuesday builds and supports my momentum for the week. It gives me that little push to move me forward.

> Giving of yourself always elevates your self-esteem.

• • • • • • •

Genuine belief in yourself and in the destiny before you is essential—but it is not blind. It necessitates two primary characteristics that will give you the **vision** you need and that are sure to make your Tuesday terrific: knowledge and assent.

Knowledge is facts, information, and skills acquired through experience or education, and it requires the theoretical understanding and practice of those elements. My ability to gather knowledge is essential as a one-on-one leadership mentor because it's all about the people I'm serving. I must determine how their personalities fit with those they are leading, and I need to discern how they can better themselves so that those around them can be better. Therefore, I focus my efforts on giving them the ability to inspect themselves so they can, as I like to say, check up from the neck up and look around from the shoulder down. I work with them to recognize and magnify their strengths while revealing and working on their problems.

Dr. Timothy Ifedioranma of Nigeria is a lawyer, pastor, bishop, and a congressperson for his country. One of my most successful leadership mentorship clients, I have visited Dr. Timothy no less than 18 times over a 20 year period. When I met with Dr. Timothy for a leadership conference in 2015, we discussed his passion to run for a seat in the Nigerian Congress. We talked about servant leadership and how that could relate to his roles in office as well as to his activities outside of the church community. We also explored how to structure his campaign. Was he going to speak solely to Christians, or was he going to try to get more people like Muslims to support his political run? He chose to be broad and invite everybody in. In Nigeria, it is common for politicians to become very wealthy. He did not want to be like them. He decided to dedicate himself to the whole community, put them first, and try to take care of all of their needs ahead of his own.

Dr. Timothy won that seat in Congress and, as of 2022, has remained in office. As I have continued to mentor him, he has done quite well and has had over 120 different churches operating under his authority. He has not only stayed the course, but he has also stayed true to his core values, who he is, and his "why" for living.

Your individual self-belief that is best supported by gaining and applying knowledge is **self-competency.** The acquisition and application of knowledge supports your self-competency by assessing your overall ability to achieve desired outcomes as well as reflect skills you can gain through study and experience to complete a goal that helps fulfill your vision.

Assent is an expression of approval or agreement, such as when two parties come together in consensus and harmony after mediation. I'll never forget when I assented to a friend so that I could learn how to best engage a specific group of business leaders. As an African American, I grew up in a culture that honors presenting yourself to others with a certain degree of confidence, even swagger. Two days prior to my presentation, I was preparing to show my consultation qualifications to members of the predominantly white business networking organization. My friend, who was white, saw me getting ready to discuss the honors and awards that I felt would validate me as a sound professional. He took me aside.

"Doc, you might not want to do it that way."

I was confused and a bit taken aback. "What do you mean?" I asked.

"They are going to think you are bragging on yourself. You're not going to convince them to work with you because they're going to think you're making it about you. They know who you are already."

I was instantly grateful, explaining to him that it is the norm in the African American culture to boldly let people know what we can do. "Matter of fact," I replied, "we give more respect to those who are doing certain things and can talk about it."

As I gave assent to my friend's sage advice, the presentation went well, the organization became a client, and the CEO of a contracting company who was at that presentation asked me to present a seminar to his team.

Your individual self-belief that is best supported by having assent is **value**. Expressing approval or agreement through assent supports value by equipping you to contribute to the cognitive, social, and moral development within a team.

Each Tuesday, I intentionally listen to or read about new leadership models or principles so that I can learn something new that I can apply to what I do. This increases my knowledge, provides opportunities to assent to new ideas, and feeds my overall vision.

* * * * * * *

Finally, your Terrific Tuesday is assured when you practice these four principles that inform and affirm your belief.

1. Reliability. Are you viewed by others as being trustworthy or as someone who consistently performs well? Being reliable to yourself and to those around you confirms your belief.

In 2018, as a new board member of the Huntsville/Madison County Chamber of Commerce, I didn't just want to hold a seat on the board. I desired to be actively involved in things. I felt that the board had done a great job in the area of economic development. However, it could improve in engaging small businesses and upstart entrepreneurs by increasing their programs to them and by letting them know they are just as important as the military installations and other large businesses in the area. I suggested they provide scholarships and discounts to small business owners and entrepreneurs who could not afford some of the chamber's programs and even offer them full membership until they could grow their enterprises.

To achieve this, I knew I had to show myself as being trustworthy to my fellow board members. I attended all of the meetings and was punctual. I constantly looked to add value to our conversations. I kept the private matters of the board confidential. My consistent commitment to operate with honesty and integrity was rewarded when I was appointed to the board's executive committee two years after first becoming a member.

The self-belief of **dependability** is confirmed when you show yourself reliable. When you gain the sense that others can depend on you, you can depend on yourself.

2. Truth. Do you live in accordance with fact or reality? What a great question—because being truthful guarantees your belief.

Back in 1996, I was a young, maturing, and idealistic leader who firmly believed that people, in general, possessed an innate longing to develop themselves. I assumed that, given the opportunity, the majority of individuals would desire to gain the knowledge and work ethic to grow and succeed. Then I offered a series of small leadership seminars on self-development in areas such as career, finance, and mindset at my church. I was hoping our congregation members would embrace the chance to engage in self-growth and share details about the seminars with their friends and in their circles of influence. I was convinced that they would eagerly and joyfully want to better themselves.

But I was shocked. The vast percentage were utterly complacent. They were comfortable to see and experience life from the bottom up.

Wow, really? I thought. *I'd be eating this up and taking advantage of it.* But they weren't. They simply didn't want to change their attitude or their position. I had to accept that.

The self-belief of **veracity** is guaranteed by being truthful. With veracity, you will see and give credence to the reality of what you and others expect in the future.

3. Ability. How do you use your talents, skills, or proficiencies to benefit yourself and others? It's not enough to have ability. Properly and humbly executing your abilities declares your belief.

In 2012, I had the privilege of traveling to Honduras with pastors and community and business leaders to speak at a crusade and leadership summit in the city of Puerto Cortés. The crystal blue waters of the Caribbean Sea provided the tropical backdrop for the outdoor portion of the event, and I marveled as the crowd gathered while kids rode bicycles or played in the dirt on the fringes. It was a large group of people, about 5,000 in all, many coming from long distances by bus.

As I spoke, an interpreter translated everything I said into Spanish. He also emulated my every movement. If I jumped, he jumped. If I spun, he spun. At one point, I took off from the stage and into the crowd, and he followed me the entire way. I was a madman, magnifying my ability to engage people and influence their behavior as I taught. Afterward, I received great feedback as many in attendance said their lives were changed for the better by what I said. Several declared that it gave them motivation and vision to pursue their dreams and goal. I was both thankful and quite humbled by it all.

The self-belief of **care** is declared by properly and humbly executing your abilities. Care brings an incredible sense of how you can help others to achieve their aspirations.

4. **Strength.** Are you able to withstand great force or pressure exerted against you? Your solidity and endurance under trial maintains your belief.

> Properly and humbly executing your abilities declares your belief.

In 2015, I came under attack as a CEO. An executive change took place at Ability Plus that upset several people. A delegation of nurses, state auditors, and even agents from the Internal Revenue Service came forth, questioning the services we were providing. The organization was investigated and scrutinized. Newly in charge, there was extraordinary pressure placed on me and my leadership team. We knew that we had been operating in integrity and firmly believed that things would eventually work out. We strongly held to our values and kept working hard and smart. In the end, we passed every audit, and the difficulties made us a better company.

The self-belief of **reliance** is maintained by being solid and having endurance under trial. You learn to hold on. It's undeniably true. You are who you are under pressure.

What do I do every Tuesday to inform and affirm my belief? In the morning, I take a moment to visit my personal goal vision board in my office at home. The white board with pictures is a visual display of my vision, and I look at it and say aloud, "This is who you are." It is a brief but consistent weekly reminder that solidifies those goals and commitments I made to myself. It makes a world of difference in terms of maintaining momentum in my mindset.

* * * * * * *

Belief has a final and enduring benefit: a recognition and release of potential. A key component of any movie worth its salt (at least by my standards) is the "chase scene." It's that vital sequence when the good guy—through extraordinary risk, daring heroics, and the gratuitous use of a stuntman—gets away from the bad guy unscathed. It's cinematic artistry.

Your week is made better by chase scenes—as long as you're the one in hot pursuit of continued progress and excellence. That requires seeing and going after your potential.

What a Wonderful Wednesday it is going to be!

[4]

WONDERFUL WEDNESDAY
Potential

"The wealthiest spot on this planet," Dr. Myles Munroe wrote in his book, *Releasing Your Potential*, "is not the oil fields of Kuwait, Iraq, or Saudi Arabia. Neither is it the gold and diamond mines of South Africa, the uranium mines of the Soviet Union, or the silver mines of Africa. Though it may surprise you, the richest deposits on our planet lie just a few blocks from your house."

Munroe then revealed that place to be the local cemetery or graveyard. There, he said, buried beneath the soil within the walls of those sacred grounds, are:

- Dreams that never came to pass.
- Songs that were never sung.
- Books that were never written.
- Paintings that never filled a canvas.
- Ideas that were never shared.
- Visions that never became reality.
- Inventions that were never designed.

- Plans that never went beyond the drawing board of the mind.
- Purposes that were never fulfilled.

"Our graveyards," he concluded, "are filled with potential that remained potential."

What wisdom! Unrealized potential is just that: unrealized.

Drawing once again from the world of science, potential energy is the prospective vitality held by an object because of its position relative to other objects, stresses within itself, or other factors. The power is there—but it is not manifested until it is released.

One comparison I like to make uses the formula for gravitational potential energy (mass x gravity x height) related to sales within a business: leads (mass) x activity (gravity) x booking appointments (height) results in sales (potential energy) being released.

Potential needs a catalyst in order to be realized. As Dr. Munroe rightly said, "A seed, until it is released, is only the promise of a tree."

In my "Point of Potential" (POP) Equation for Success seminars, I take out an apple, cut it in half to expose the seeds at the core, and hold it out to the audience. "We all see this apple," I teach, "but it came from a seed. Inside each seed is a tree, and inside a tree are more apples. Everything starts from the seed, and it is the seed that has the potential to produce a tree that will produce more apples."

"If the seed is not placed into the ground where it can germinate and be watered and nourished, it does not grow. It's promised potential is not released," I tell attendees. "That means we have to plant the seeds of potential that reside at our core.

WONDERFUL WEDNESDAY – POTENTIAL

We have to water ourselves through trainings, research, study, and education. We have to sacrifice. Only then can a tree grow. Then, when it does, there will be a time that tree will need to be pruned. We will need to cut back, getting rid of anything or anyone that isn't doing us any good, in order to bear more fruit."

The POP equation I created is **S + WE x W = POP**—or **S**tart + **W**ork **E**thic x **W**hy = **P**oint **o**f **P**otential. Potential always starts somewhere. My start traces all the way back to growing up in the projects and living in government housing in small town Alabama. When I was 15, I was sitting in the kitchen one afternoon with my mother, Johnnie, when she planted the seed of potential in my life. She was cooking,

> **S + WE x W = POP**– or **S**tart + **W**ork **E**thic x **W**hy = **P**oint **o**f **P**otential.

and I was telling her how I was thinking about becoming a doctor. She was a nurse, and I had been reading her medical books with keen interest.

"Karockas," she declared, "you are smart. You can be anything in the world—except president of the United States. Do not let what you see dictate what you could be."

That was quite the proclamation to make back then to an African American boy from the projects, and I can't help but laugh today at her qualifier: Barack Obama has proven that even our nation's highest political office can be attained by a person of color.

My mother's words encouraged me, and though I did not become a doctor, I have attained a doctorate—and achieved so much more than even I thought possible in my roles as a pastor, business leader, and entrepreneur. I may not have had many of the advantages other people have enjoyed, but I had a launching pad, thanks to my mother. I used it to motivate myself.

That said, I still had to take my start and add a relentless work ethic multiplied by my fully defined "why" (to lead, teach, train, and empower people to reach their destiny by helping them to maximize their potential) in order to reach my own Point of Potential—that place where my potential was released and became a reality.

....

On Sunday, we began the week by establishing our vision. We set our attitude on Monday and infused our belief on Tuesday. What better way, then, to meet and overcome the traditional "hump" day of Wednesday and make it wonderful than by igniting and fulfilling our potential?

Once more, your mindset is key; specifically, one of meditation where you focus your thoughts to see and rehearse the actions you want. When you are truly *present* with your mindset, you'll discover that your brain can hardly tell the difference between what you rehearse in advance and experience in real time. One automatically feeds the other.

There are five attributes of a Wonderful Wednesday that will foster your meditation and direct you toward the release of your potential.

1. Train your brain not to be a record of your past, but a map to your future

Our brains record information that is stored in our conscience until we are challenged or called upon to use it. When that happens, many recall negative messages—"You can't do this." "This is too hard." "No one has ever done that before." "My family failed at this, so I will, too."—which cause them to feel average and often places them on a path of failure.

Therefore, you must place new, positive information into the hard drive of your brain that foretells and inspires your success and maps out your brighter future. "Nothing can stop me. I can do all things!" "Greatness is inside of me. It will just take some work to get it out of me." "I will look at every hill as something I can get over." "If I keep moving forward, I will profit from it sooner or later."

Though challenges are inevitable, this new mapping of your brain shows that you have or will overcome, conquer, and succeed. One of the most remarkable things you have the power to do is literally *rewrite* your brain. Scientists refer to this as neuroplasticity: the ability of neural networks in the brain to change through growth and reorganization in response to new situations or to changes in their environment. For example, when individuals with an addictive behavior make consistent, ongoing alterations in their thinking and behavior, the brain closes down the old neural pathways that enabled that addiction and opens up new neural pathways that support ongoing sobriety or abstinence.

More than mere willpower, your positive thoughts and choices rewrite your brain. As this happens, your brain heals itself!

How does this work? As a church pastor, I faced a situation where I had to train my brain to not be a record of the past. We needed to move to a new, bigger location. Anytime we had done this before, the move met with much pain and disappointment. People left. Tithes and offerings decreased. Many who stayed didn't feel we needed to make the change because they were very comfortable where they were. Everything was received by the congregation as a negative—and that stuck in my brain. I was overwhelmed with anxiety, and I even wondered if everyone was going to leave this time.

I had to change my mindset and see the church relocation in a positive, successful way in order to create a map of progress toward the future. Three times every week, I went to the new building, sat in my car, and meditated. Next, I walked inside and went into every classroom, envisioning the teaching that was going to take place. I stood in the main sanctuary and imagined the messages to come and how they were going to be received with enthusiasm. I went beyond visualization, speaking aloud the positives I wanted to see happen in each and every space in that building. I saw our people joyful, happy, and embracing the move as an opportunity for us to expand our outreach and grow in our faith.

As I did this, my brain's neural pathways changed. Negative thinking was vanquished. Positive thinking was established. That influenced how I felt and behaved. Today, my church is thriving, and I continue to walk through the building once a week meditating and speaking out loud. I call into existence those things which be not as though they were, and I declare that a positive future will come to pass.

2. Teach your body what the future feels like emotionally ahead of the actual experience

In addition to addressing our thoughts and behavior, we must train ourselves emotionally. This improves our self-esteem: how we feel about ourselves.

Incredibly, the average person has as many as 60,000 thoughts a day—and the vast majority of them, 80 percent, are negative.[6] You can offset this trend in your thinking by emotionally esteeming your current goals and your future expectations about them above your present reality. See it, believe it, and act as if it has already happened. Tell yourself, "Yes, I can! I can feel this way. I *deserve* to feel this way."

Self-esteem is your subjective evaluation of your own worth. It encompasses your self-beliefs as impacted by emotional states such as pleasure, triumph, pride, despair, shame, and pain. In their 2007 article on the Rosenberg Self-Esteem Scale Greek Validation on Student Sample, Eliot R. Smith and Diane M. Mackie explained that "self-concept is what we think about the self; self-esteem is the positive or negative evaluations of the self, as in how we feel about it."[7]

I'll never forget my first board meeting as CEO at Ability Plus. My body was feeling so much anxiety about what could go wrong. The organization had been in disarray. The previous leader had not been forthright with the board. They were having a crisis of trust. Previously, board meetings had involved long hours of bickering. The overall culture was bad from all of the dysfunction, and I was still feeling disappointed and frustrated about all of this stemming from my time as the organization's chief operating officer. As CEO, I was in a position to change things and make a difference, but I was nervous and fearful.

So, I had to refocus my energy and mindset to believe and experience a positive, productive meeting before it occurred. As I had as pastor at the church, I meditated for about 15 minutes the night before the board meeting and again about an hour before the start of the meeting. I went into the boardroom and thought about how fun and productive it was going to be. I pictured smiles on everyone's faces. I engaged the theater of my mind to visualize a positive outcome. That changed my emotional outlook.

That first meeting went well, and the board meetings that followed it got even better. We went to work to reform damaged processes, rebuild broken trust, and change the culture. It worked—but it all started as I taught my body what the future felt like emotionally ahead of the actual experience.

3. Transform your attitude to feel empowered even when you have not received recognition.

It's easy to wait for someone to provide us with a sense of accomplishment before we feel good about our ability, efficiency, or strength. But it's far better to see yourself as accomplished and empowered on the canvas of your imagination before the success is manifested. That way, you will feel that the capability is inside of you from the very start.

> It's far better to see yourself as accomplished and empowered on the canvas of your imagination.

When I launched my work as a leadership consultant, I knew that I had to feel capable of doing a great job before I ever did a single seminar or coaching session. I could not afford to wait until someone said, "Good job, Karockas." I needed to feel empowered that a good job was going to happen. Once more, it started with meditation. Many times, I envisioned myself commanding a crowd like Les Brown or engaging an audience like John C. Maxwell. I'd tell myself, *They can't beat Doc Rock!* I saw myself walking off stage with people saying, "Man, that dude was awesome!"

This did not flow from any sense of arrogance. It came solely from the perspective of building my self-awareness and self-confidence. In doing so, the aspect of my potential that I released was open-mindedness. I believed and felt that I was capable of consulting and coaching, and that transformation of my attitude contributed to my success.

4. Conform your mindset to feel abundant before you receive wealth.

It's also just as easy to wait until our bank account, assets, environment, or social circles look more favorable before we feel we are abundant. That doesn't need to be the case. Your abundance can be experienced in the mind before it is played out on the daily court of life. You can walk with your head up and your shoulders back as you develop a holistic sense of abundance in advance so that you feel you have everything you need to achieve what you want.

In 2013, I felt that the church I was leading had to alter some essential outreach philosophies to become more inclusive. I wanted to present our ministry from a more contemporary point of view, reaching people where they were with grace and love instead of with judgment. Vast numbers of the congregation, however, favored tradition and did not want to change. As they left the church, giving dramatically decreased, leaving it in a financial bind.

Yet even with our monetary abundance threatened, I refused to go forward with a mindset of lack. I told myself each day that the condition of our cash flow was great and that we were going to experience more opportunity and prosperity as we stayed the course. Over time, that is exactly what happened.

5. Adjust your awareness to feel accepted and respected even when others haven't made you feel that way.

All of us like to "feel the love" from those around us, so much so that we may wait to feel that way about ourselves until someone else shows it to us. But you should accept and respect yourself anyway without having to feel loved by others, acting as if you have already received that appreciation.

I recall struggling with this early in my business consultation career. I wanted to be loved by others, especially those I perceived as being ahead of me. When I didn't readily "feel the love," it fostered doubt in my mind. *Am I supposed to be in this room? Does everybody want me to be here? Do I deserve to be here?* I had to act as though I knew I was supposed to be in the room. *I'm* here, I told myself. *I can't wait for them to come over to me. I have to believe and behave as if everybody is waiting to hear my name, talk to me, and ask questions about my expertise.* Acceptance and respect had to come from me first. I had to give both to myself.

Did I ever have to overcome a sense that I was only pretending to feel loved or "faking it 'til I made it?" Sure, a little bit. But in the end, I came to the awareness that my inner acceptance and self-respect were real and just as significant as though I'd received it from others. Of course, there were those who let me "feel the love," and that was great. But I got to the point where I didn't need that in order to feel like I belonged with those people.

Every Wednesday morning and evening, I foster meditation and direct myself toward the release of my potential by taking time to look at my vision board and think about the grand scale items such as a leadership development center for Vision Excellence Company, tripling company growth for Ability Plus, a new ministry facility for my church, and getting and keeping myself in great physical shape. I see these goals as though they were already completed so that I can share the benefits of those achievements with others.

In my meditation, I use verbalization, visualization, and internalization. These three encompass and address the basic components of an *experience* shaped by words spoken out loud, emotions felt as real, and images seen on the canvas of my imagination. I am convinced that experiences such as these have the most potent impact on the belief system that controls our lives.

* * * * * * *

What is excellence? It is the quality of being outstanding, truly the best, at everything you do. A child prodigy on the violin,

Joshua Bell became a world-class musician at the young age of 29. Raised in the American heartland, Joshua always endeavored to be his best—at music, computers, chess, even video games. He pushed himself to excel. One day, while visiting his hometown of Bloomington, Indiana, a small boy approached him.

"You're Joshua Bell," he exclaimed. "You're famous!"

Joshua humbly responded, "Well, not really."

But the boy was insistent. "Yes, really! Your name is on every video game in the arcade as the highest scorer!"

Different people measure excellence in different ways, but it is always that which sets its standard for a particular area—and the characteristics of a Wonderful Wednesday designed to release your potential revolve around your own pursuit of excellence.

Be intentional by allocating attention to your purpose. Your purpose—your "why" in life that is centered around your gifts and passions—does not just happen. It is something that requires your daily attention. When you allocate time to do what is needed to pursue your purpose, you automatically unleash your potential and accelerate toward excellence. One great way to do this is to daily review and speak your purpose out loud.

I remember being in an executive staff meeting where we discussed the industry standard for business excellence. I noted how many companies were being allowed to operate with low excellence in the area of professionalism. We decided that, though apathy was an easier path, we wanted to do everything we could to operate at the highest level of professional excellence.

We developed a strategy to be the most professional company in our industry. Surprisingly, we were confronted by naysayers who mistakenly thought we were just trying to make ourselves seem more "special" than our competitors. These naysayers had a lack of confidence, purpose, and direction that caused them to think the way that they did. Yet it was not our intention to put anyone down. We simply wanted to set the bar high for ourselves and go after it. As a result, our executive team was challenged to look at average as the enemy to great, and their mindsets changed to look, act, and move toward being the very best.

Be expectant by aiming past your expectations. I've always said, "Shoot for the galaxies and maybe you will land on the moon." It's an attitude that came from being raised near Huntsville, Alabama, also known as the "Rocket City" because it is the home of the United States Space and Rocket Center, the National Aeronautics and Space Administration's Marshall Space Flight Center, and the United States Army Aviation and Missile Command. It's always been a place where progressive industries in aerospace, defense, and biotech have informed its culture.

As a kid, I remember going to the Space and Rocket Center during an all-day, fifth grade field trip. I didn't know it was a replica then, but I was amazed when I saw the Saturn 5 rocket that took us to the moon towering high into the crystal blue Alabama sky. When the tour guides spoke about how everyone at the Space and Rocket Center had to be innovative in technology and communications, something was stirred within me to think that nothing was impossible. They went beyond the limits of what many expected in sending humans to the moon. Why couldn't I do the same in my life?

I've found that many people tend to set their goals so low they can't help but hit them all. However, to unleash your potential and achieve excellence, you

> To unleash your potential and achieve excellence, you must stretch yourself above and beyond.

must stretch yourself above and beyond where you think you can go. When I first began speaking internationally, my goals could've been seen as unrealistic for a young man raised in government housing. I wanted to travel to 50 countries around the world. It all started in Nigeria in 1998 when I was asked to speak at a ministry conference there. As of the beginning of 2022, I had spoken in no fewer than 31 countries such as China, Spain, Honduras, the United Kingdom, Kenya, Brazil, and Israel, conducting leadership seminars and conferences. Today, I am planning the next level of services—mentorship, executive coaching, and business development—with the goal of going to places I've never been before like Australia, Indonesia, and Sweden, endeavoring to reach that milestone of 50 nations by 2032.

Be proactive by having a strong vision for the long term. You must constantly be on high alert with your vision. Why? Because vision always puts you beyond your capacity, but never beyond your potential to see, plan, and produce your desired future with imagination. After all, Albert Einstein said, "Imagination is everything. It is the preview to life's coming attractions,"[8] while George Washington Carver stated, "Where there is no vision, there is no hope."[9] When you are proactive with your vision, it gives you renewed hope to keep pressing toward your potential.

As CEO of Ability Plus, I was proactive with the vision I had of owning our own building with offices and a career center. We had rented building space for years, and even during hard times with our operations and finances, we kept the vision to own at the forefront. In 2017, we purchased our own building that provided us with the necessary offices, meeting rooms, and campus space that we didn't have before, enabling us not just to continue but to expand our mission to those we serve.

Be thirsty to invest in your capacity by obtaining, retaining, and improving your knowledge and skills. Continual education and self-improvement are essential to growing toward the fulfillment of your potential. It is necessary that you stay on top of industry changes and embrace a growth mindset at all costs.

I had already obtained several degrees when I decided to enter the graduate school business and leadership certificate program at Vanderbilt University in 2015. Some people insisted that I already had enough education—and that may have been true. But I didn't have the proper knowledge that was necessary to get me to the next level in my potential. Through this program, I received training in conflict resolution, change management, and other critical skills. I also gained additional business and leadership acumen.

To promote the pursuit of excellence in my life, I make sure I learn something new each and every Wednesday. It may be small, and it doesn't take much time from the day, but it is always something that I know will improve and extend my skills.

....

Once you have begun using meditation and focusing on excellence to release your potential in the middle of your work week, the last way to guarantee a Wonderful Wednesday is by doing everything you can to inspire your productivity by following these three principles.

1. Limit your external distractions.

Two Major League Baseball hall of famers—Yogi Berra, catcher for the New York Yankees, and Hank Aaron, home run hitting king for the Milwaukee Braves, were playing in the 1957

World Series. Berra, who was notorious for his ceaseless chatter, used to pick up his teammates while distracting the opposing team's batters. As Aaron came up to the plate, Berra said, "Henry, you're holding the bat wrong. You're supposed to hold it so you can read the trademark."

Aaron didn't say anything. Instead, he slammed the next pitch into the left field bleachers. After rounding the bases and stepping on home plate, Aaron looked at Berra. "I didn't come up here to read," he said.[10]

Hank Aaron would not be distracted from the task at hand, and neither should you. I have put into practice four easy to understand (yet difficult to execute) ways to limit distractions.

a. Manage your phone/tablet/laptop: Treat your electronic devices primarily as a tool for productivity, not an instrument of entertainment. Most of us have a tendency to be distracted and amused by our devices, often utilizing them as stress releasers. That's why it is best to purposefully curtail entertainment and target using your devices on tasks that help you achieve your goals and dreams. This is hard to do because it decreases the feeling of satisfaction and comfort you get when devices are employed for other purposes.

b. Manage people: Always be open and show respect to everyone, but don't allow anyone to control or misuse your time. Many people have good intentions but are bad time managers when interacting with others. Yet you must manage every relationship with respect to the milestones and priorities at hand. This is difficult because we generally don't want others to think that we don't care about them or don't want to take time for their concerns.

c. Manage your work and study space: Work is the necessary activity that enables you to achieve success, so it must be given proper precedence and respect. Your work or study space must be guarded as the sanctuary it is to get this activity moving and keep it going. This is not easy to do because other things tend to come up to interrupt or supersede your prioritization of work and study.

d. Manage noise: Noise comes your way every day, usually in the form of people or fun, and it clamors for your time and attention. The best way to silence it is to intentionally review your daily tasks and see what goals need to be accomplished to fulfill those tasks. As you keep the big picture in front of you, you are able to give it preference over the noise. This is difficult because it requires great discipline.

2. Identify your priorities.

"A weakness of all human beings," inventor and entrepreneur Henry Ford once stated, "is trying to do too many things at once. That scatters effort and destroys direction. It makes for haste, and haste makes waste. So, we do things all the wrong ways possible before we come to the right one. Every now and then, I wake up in the morning headed toward that finality with a dozen things I want to do. I know I can't do them all at once."

When asked what he did about that, Ford replied, "I go out and trot around the house. While I'm running off the excess energy that wants to do too much, my mind clears, and I see what can be done and should be done first."[11]

Knowing how to pinpoint and do "first things first" is essential to setting your priorities—and I've learned that the ABCDE Method is a powerful priority setting technique that you can use every single day. Basically, it is a to-do list on steroids, and its power lies in its simplicity because it's so action oriented. All you do is start with a list of everything you want to accomplish for the coming day, then employ the ABCDE Method.

"A" items are most important.
"B" items only have minor consequences.
"C" tasks have no consequences.
"D" indicates items you can delegate.
"E" shows tasks that you can eliminate.

In my office at the start of each day, I look at my action items and break them down into four categories: three for the organizations that I lead and one for personal tasks. Next, I prioritize each list using ABCDE. This can get tricky because each ranking is based on the various criticalities, the items of extreme importance, for that given day. This is vital because each day is different and fluid. Something categorized as "C" yesterday might be an "A" today. Unexpected meetings or events can become more important that other action items. Dealing with such criticalities and the fluidity of each individual day is the strength of the ABCDE Method. It becomes a tool that allows you to have the flexibility you need to be most productive.

3. Have a method for measuring productivity.

Former athlete Deion Sanders once played as an outfielder for the Atlanta Braves and a cornerback for the Atlanta Falcons at the same time. He is the only athlete to have hit a home run in Major League Baseball and scored a touchdown in the National Football League in the same week—so he knows a little something about productivity.

While growing up in Fort Myers, Florida, Sanders met several would-be athletes. "I call them Idas," he said. "'If I'da done this, I'd be making three million today,' or 'If I'da practiced a little harder, I'd be a superstar.' They were as fast as me when they were kids, but instead of working for their dreams, they chose drugs and a life of street corners. When I was young,

I had practice; my friends who didn't went straight to the streets and never left." He concluded, "We don't need any more Idas."[12]

You'll know that you are being productive—and not being another "Ida"—by employing these methods to track your productivity.

- Establish a baseline.
- Define and measure tasks.
- Set clear objectives and goals.
- Identify benchmarks and targets.
- Follow your individual progress.

At General Motors, I oversaw a project to retool an assembly line with electric torque guns so that they would be implemented on two of the three standard work shifts: day, evening, and overnight. Much had to be done in the established baseline of three months to complete the first phase of the retooling, from training to the ordering and installation of equipment. We set weekly benchmarks for everyone, and I had to keep an overall log of activities to monitor our progress and keep us on schedule. All five tracking methods were employed.

There were a few unforeseen challenges that arose from some of the workers being skeptical of the new process, but we overcame them by listening to one another, asking and answering detailed questions, and working together. The project was fully and successfully completed within the baseline.

·······

In the end, I plug all of these things into my personal POP equation to continually strive for my Point of Potential. As a result, I don't just get over my "hump" days—I launch over them like a kid speeding his bike to a hill and ramping himself up and beyond it.

Yet there are days, more than I'd like to admit, where I need an infusion of confidence to make it through to the other side—and that is where your Triumphant Thursday comes into play.

[5]

TRIUMPHANT THURSDAY
Confidence

Confidence can come from something tangible. The noted American artist, John Singer Sargent, was considered the leading portrait painter of his generation, creating nearly 900 oil paintings and more than 2,000 watercolors, as well as countless sketches and charcoal drawings. He once painted a panel of roses that was highly praised by critics. A small picture, Sargent was offered a high price for it on many occasions, but he refused to sell it. He considered it his best work and was very proud of it.

Whenever he was deeply discouraged and doubtful of his abilities as an artist, he would look at it and remind himself, "I painted that." Then his confidence and ability would come back to him.[13]

Confidence can also come from an unwavering mindset. John McKay, a well-known college and professional football coach for over 25 years, wrote about the supreme confidence of legendary University of Alabama football coach Bear Bryant. "We were out shooting ducks, and finally, after about three hours, here comes one lonely duck. The Bear fires. And that duck is still flying today. But Bear watched the duck flap away, looked at me and said, 'John, you are witnessing a genuine miracle. There flies a dead duck!'"[14]

Confidence is the feeling or belief that you can do something well or succeed. Yet research shows few people are born confident. One study, from geneticist and psychologist Robert Plomin, makes an argument that some people may get a genetic boost toward confidence.[15] He researched 15,000 sets of twins in Britain, testing them in three academic subjects (math, writing, and science), then asking them to rate how confident they were about their abilities in each subject. He theorized that genetics have an impact on confidence (as defined by your perceived ability to do well) of up to 50 percent while the rest is affected by environment, experiences, and upbringing. Plomin's study clearly showed that believing you will succeed is a reliable predictor of actually doing so.

Truth is, the confident person learns to be that way—and you can, too.

Confident belief is essential. Why? Coach, self-improvement thought leader, and author Barrie Davenport points out, "Low confidence makes us doubt our abilities and judgment and prevents us from taking calculated risks, setting ambitious goals, and acting on them."[16] Yet having confident belief positions you to succeed and lead. Lawyer and businessman Clarence B. Randall once said, "The leader must know that he knows, and be able to make it abundantly clear to those around him that he knows."[17]

> Truth is, the confident person learns to be that way.

Confidence killers

Confidence is a cornerstone of leadership. It is also the incubator for the embryo of your dreams and the birthplace of your destiny. But in order to learn and develop the triumphant confidence you desire, you will need to confront and overcome three confidence killers.

Killer 1: Low self-esteem.

The self-defeating thought, "I don't think I can," rises from a deeper, more destructive belief that says, "I don't think I *am*." This causes you to more easily give up trying to get what you want.

I understand how paralyzing low self-esteem can be. Early in my time at General Motors, I was made the lead project engineer of the rack and pinion steering gear line, taking over for a gentleman who had been there four times as long as I had. The cost, responsibility, and overall care of this line was critically important to the well-being of the entire plant. To say that I was nervous is an understatement, but I had to find the confidence deep within to meet the responsibility given to me. I spoke self-assuring words to myself, focusing on positive outcomes for the production line. Whenever doubts arose, I put my mind on achieving high results. Above average was the minimum I would accept.

It turned out that I remained in that position for the next five years. The line was very successful, and I ended up being promoted to another plant to take over a half shaft line as project manager.

Killer 2: Fear.

I believe it was the great motivational speaker, author, and sales expert Zig Ziglar who popularized the compelling acronym for fear as being False Evidence Appearing Real—and I have found that acronym to be undeniably true.

I can trace two specific fears back to my childhood: the fear of loud noises and the fear of falling. One day when I was seven, I was visiting my granddad, and a fire truck zoomed by with its siren wailing as I was playing outside. For some reason, I thought the engine was trying to get me—and I scrambled so fast to run away from it that I hit my head on the brick corner of the apartment building. I had to get stitches, and I still bear the scar from the injury. I told my mother what happened, and about three months later, she took me to visit someone she knew who worked at a fire station. He took us inside, got up in the fire truck, and turned on the siren. I was afraid at first and felt like running away once more. But after a few moments, I realized the truck was not trying to get me. The fire engine wasn't a bad thing at all.

My fear of falling came from dreams I had as a child. In them, I always fell off a high cliff. I could see and feel myself plummeting toward the earth, but I would never reach it. I just kept helplessly tumbling through the air. I overcame this fear by imagining myself landing safely on my feet as if I were Superman coming in for a landing.

I have discovered five practical ways you can conquer your fears.

1. Practice reacting aggressively and positively toward the fears in your imagination: As you do this, it will be just a matter of time before those mental reactions extend into your physical world and become a reality in your actual life. As soon as you identify a negative thought creeping into your mind, change your internal dialogue to reverse the thought and put a positive spin to it. Replace irrational "what ifs" with "I'll handle it," "It can be done," or "I'll figure it out."

2. Change the atmosphere: Take risks, and set out to do what your heart desires. As Lee Ann Womack sang, "When you get the choice to sit it out or dance, I hope you dance." Despite my earlier success as a student, when I was at Kettering University, I possessed an abiding fear of taking tests. I was nervous and scared that I wouldn't do my best. I conquered this with a little role play. I dressed in a business suit and tie. I may have looked different than my classmates on test days, but in that attire, I felt like I was getting down to business. I'd sit down at my desk convinced that it was time to *take care* of business! The technique worked brilliantly.

The single most important thing you can do to build self-confidence is to actually go out and *do* what you fear. Afraid to fly? Take a short flight with a trusted friend. Scared of heights? Go to the upper floor of a building and stay near the window for a spell. Claustrophobic? Take a favorite book or music with you, turn on the light, and sit in your closet. Safely but boldly face your fears.

3. Act as if it is impossible to fail: When you know that it can be done, you can invoke the ability already within you that will enable you to do it. If a mistake happens along the way, don't dwell on it. Just correct your actions as you go along.

4. Relax your fear away: Psychological studies suggest that it is not possible for you to feel fear when the muscles of your body are perfectly relaxed. So, the moment you recognize that anxiety is creeping in and your muscles start to tighten up, focus on loosening them. Meditation is an excellent tool to combat and conquer fear.

5. Substitute the feeling of fear with another positive, "feel good" feeling: Think about anything that strikes a chord and leaves you with a pleasant sensation. Capture that feeling and use it to replace your fear.

A good friend of mine was going in for an MRI and knew he'd feel uncomfortable being inside the tube of the machine. It made him feel trapped like a cork in a bottle. What did he do? During the entire 20 minute procedure, he closed his eyes and envisioned himself at a wide open baseball stadium watching a game with his grandchild, reliving a treasured memory of a past event and experiencing how it made him feel: happy and peaceful. He made it through the MRI without having to even think about hitting the panic button.

Killer 3: Other people's opinions of you.
If you worry about what other people think of you, it is because you have placed more confidence in them and their opinions than in yourself.

When I first got started in motivational speaking and facilitating leadership trainings, I was criticized by a gentleman who was a leader and well-known speaker in the community. He told me point blank that I was not a good speaker because I did not enunciate my words properly and spoke too fast. At first, I entertained what he said—but I quickly realized that I had been given a special gift from God to engage and share with others. I concluded that his opinion was just that, an opinion, which ultimately had no bearing on who I was and what I was striving to become.

· · · · · · ·

Triumphant Attributes and Traits

Thursday is uniquely positioned in the work week. It's not quite Friday yet, but you can feel it, right? The conclusion of the week is near. Saturday and the weekend are not that far away.

As much as Wednesday is the mid-week "hump" day, Thursday is that day when you feel you are starting to turn the corner toward the finish line.

There's an anticipation to Thursday that makes you want to do everything in your power to make it positive and, well, triumphant—and here are four great attributes, followed by four key traits, that make that possible.

1. It's a day to begin with the end in mind.
Thursday is a perfect day to know what you want to accomplish from the very beginning. That way, everything else you do can leads you to where you want to go.

One summer, my staff and I at Ability Plus were dealing with a daunting challenge to finalize our detailed policies and procedures in order to accommodate new government guidelines for our organization. One specific Thursday, I woke up with extra anticipation that we were going to accomplish our assignment. I was determined to see the end of the exercise fulfilled, and the sunny, beautiful morning fed my optimism. I knew the day was going to be long and tedious with a lot of work ahead, but I saw the finish line. That day ended up being pivotal to us completing the policies and procedures. Shortly after that, we were able to put the final period on the last sentence of the project.

2. It's a day to put your thoughts in their place.
If you place your hand over an open flame, your brain responds so that you won't do that again. But that survival mechanism can also work against you because it causes you to focus on the negative rather than the positive. Therefore, you want to train your brain to emphasize the good over the bad in whatever

situations you face. Here are some simple yet profound ways you can do just that.

Forget each kindness that you do as soon as you have done it.

Forget the praise that falls to you the moment you have won it.

Forget the slander that you hear before you can repeat it.

Forget each slight, each spite, each sneer, whenever you may meet it.

Remember every promise made and keep it to the letter.

Remember those who lend you aid and be a grateful debtor.

Remember all the happiness that comes your way in living.

Forget each worry and distress; be hopeful and forgiving.

Remember good, remember truth, remember to love those around you.

And you will find, through age and youth, that many will love you, too.[18]

3. It's a day to take control of self-talk.

How often do you speak powerful, positional words to yourself? Like the prize fighter who looks in the mirror and declares himself to be a champion before entering the ring, you should motivate yourself to excel and win!

I was scheduled to do the keynote address at the NAVIGATE Nonprofit Network Conference 2022 in Huntsville, Alabama. The premier conference in the region for nonprofit leaders, boards, and their supporters with over 600 participants, my address took place on a Thursday. Before heading to the stage, I looked in a mirror. "You got this!" I told myself. "Go out there and 'Doc Rock 'Em!'" The keynote went wonderfully, I had a great time, and even the mayor of the city was excited by my presentation.

4. It's a day to expand beyond your comfort zone.

When you intentionally step outside your comfort zone, it expands. If we stay within it, that zone eventually starts to shrink. You will avoid this by pushing yourself to do things that stretch you and even involve some risk.

> When you intentionally step outside your comfort zone, it expands.

When I was a young engineer, I wasn't very comfortable speaking to executives about a project. So, when several executives came from headquarters to look at new projects and processes that we had been working on at the Saginaw division of General Motors, I was quite nervous and did everything I could to get out of the presentation. I thought my manager, or another teammate, could do it for me. But instead of running from the situation and my responsibility, I mustered up the courage to push myself to give the presentation anyway. My managers and others were very satisfied with it, giving me a new sense of confidence that I had never experienced before and that still carries over today.

The four common traits of the person who makes Thursdays triumphant emphasize a willingness to seek assistance and to have resilience.

Trait 1. Ask for help.

A three-year-old girl was getting ready to head upstairs to get ready for bed when she asked her father to come with her to help.

"You know how to undress yourself," her dad gently reminded her.

"Yes," she explained, "but sometimes people need people anyway, even if they know how to do things themselves."

Smiling, the dad followed his girl up to her room, thankful for the lesson on helpfulness she had given him.[19] The child didn't assume her father knew what she wanted. She made her request for help, and her reason for wanting it, clear.

It may be for their expertise or just their presence—but be ready to let other people know what you want—because once they know you want their help, you will be surprised at how forthcoming and appreciative they are to provide it.

Trait 2. Find a mentor.
Whatever you've set out to do, there are likely others who've done it first and can offer you useful advice or serve as a role model. Find those people and learn as much as you can from them.

The greatest mentor in my life was Dr. Maurice K. Wright. When I was starting my assignment as CEO of Ability Plus, he offered me wisdom that gave me both leadership direction and stability. I had an issue with a group of individuals who were trying to hurt me and the company. They not only harshly criticized what we were doing, but they claimed that we were lying about our processes and that they were not up to state standards. It made me angry, and I really wanted to retaliate and go after them.

Yet there's a reason I say that everyone needs a "Dr. Wright!" He mentored me through the ordeal, meeting with me on a weekly basis. He identified my blind spots, such as letting my emotions take over. He pointed out that if I kept being good, moving forward, and doing the right things, I would prevail. With Dr. Wright's counsel, direction, and patience, both me and the company came to a positive outcome from the situation.

Trait 3. Get ready to bounce back.

It's not failure that destroys your confidence, and it's not getting back up. Failure is an ingredient in the process of success. Once you get back up, you've learned what doesn't work and can give it another try. Don't allow anything to keep you from reaching your desired destination.

Everybody recognizes that Ludwig van Beethoven was a musical genius. But few realize the adversity he had to overcome to achieve greatness. In his twenties, Beethoven began to lose his hearing. The problem haunted him into the middle years of his life, but he kept it a guarded secret. By the time he reached his fifties, Beethoven was completely deaf. But he refused to give up. He was once overheard shouting at the top of his voice, "I will take life by the throat!" Many of his biographers believe the only reason Beethoven remained productive for so long was his undaunted determination to bounce back.[20]

Trait 4. Choose your companions wisely.

Your general outlook, negative or positive, will reflect the cumulative average perspective of the five people you spend the most time with—so make sure you're hanging out with people who encourage you and lift you up. The opinions of others matter and speak to your feelings, which will impact your confidence.

In my book *God-A-Tude* published in 2021, I mentioned an old saying of mine: "I don't hang with chickens. I eat chicken, but I hang with eagles." I have a group of leaders in my life—men and women who own companies, build people, and show care for society— and I call them "eagles." Each one of these five people have shown me how to keep fighting and to win. One of them once challenged me to do better during a staff meeting by asking me to look at financial data a little deeper and trim some things to reduce the budget and improve overall stewardship of our funds.

It was tough. I wasn't expecting it, and it upset me at first. Yet he told me, "If you keep questioning your decisions, you'll never be great." He challenged me to never accept average and to have the confidence that I could do whatever I worked to do. I accepted his direction, reworked the budget, and everyone was better for it.

· · · · · · ·

Defining principles

The fourth day of the workweek can have its downside, though. As much as it is a day for anticipation, it can also be a day that easily gives way to apathy. Perhaps you're feeling weary and can't wait for the week to end and the weekend to arrive. You can let down your guard and decrease your effort and focus.

Here is a trio of preparation principles that, when you allow them to define your Triumphant Thursday, will keep such indifference at bay.

Do your homework.

Preparation will help boost your confidence. Have to give a speech? Practice it several times, record yourself, and listen. Meeting people for the first time? Learn more about them and their organizations in advance. Facing a challenging assignment? Do your research.

Several centuries ago, a Japanese emperor commissioned an artist to paint a bird. A number of months passed, but still no painting was brought to the palace. Finally, the emperor became so exasperated that he went to the artist's home to demand an explanation.

Instead of making excuses, the artist placed a blank canvas on the easel. In less than an hour, he completed the painting that went on to become a brilliant masterpiece. When the emperor asked the reason for the delay, the artist showed him armloads of drawings of feathers, wings, heads, and feet. Then he explained that all of that research and study was necessary before he could begin and complete the painting.[21]

Get plenty of rest and exercise.
There's ample evidence that sleep, exercise, and good nutrition profoundly affects both your mood and your effectiveness. Moderate exercise just three times a week for 20 minutes each time does much to fight depression and maintain a positive attitude of success and confidence.

Once I began coaching and consulting, I decided that if I was going to teach others to be disciplined and to reach their dreams, I had to be disciplined with my own physical fitness. Each morning, I began exercising for at least 15 minutes. That eventually developed into a daily 30-minute regimen of push-ups, sit ups, squats, leg kicks, and dumbbell work. I don't go to a gym. I have an area in my home office for these activities—an area where I have a big fabric banner someone gave to me that declares, "No Bad Days!" I've found it is very refreshing to accomplish a physical feat early in the morning. It's a way that I say to each day, "Let's go!"

Align your intention with your impact.
I came across a story about two men who went hunting. Neither one was a terribly good shot, so after they had tramped through

the fields for hours, they had yet to hit anything. With evening coming on, both were getting tired. One turned to the other and said, "What about it? Let's just miss two more and call it a day." Despite the lack of anything to show for their time, the two hunters probably expended as much energy and effort as if they had been successful.

The same thing can happen to you. "It is not enough to be busy," someone once said. "One must also get results."[22] Figure out the impact that you want to make in a given situation and align your intentions with the results of that impact. Be intentional in all that you do!

* * * * * * *

A pompous young man once came to the great philosopher, Socrates, asking for knowledge. Socrates recognized the type of person he was dealing with and led the young man through the streets, to the sea, and then chest deep into the water. "What do you want?" Socrates asked.

"Knowledge, O wise Socrates," said the young man with a proud smile.

Socrates put his strong hands on the man's shoulders—and promptly pushed him under water. Thirty seconds later, Socrates let him up. "What do you want?" he asked again.

"Knowledge," the young man gasped.

Socrates sent him under again. Thirty more seconds passed before Socrates pulled the young man's head above the waves.

"What do you want, young man?"

Between heavy, heaving breaths, the humbled fellow wheezed. "Air!" he screeched. "I need air!"

Socrates put a supporting arm around the man. "When you want knowledge as much as you just wanted air, then you will have it."[23]

Socrates knew that the young man needed to have the appropriate *enthusiasm* about what he wanted, above all else, in order to have the *drive* to go after it and get it—and so do you. That's why I've made enthusiasm and drive the keynote of a Fantastic Friday!

[6]

FANTASTIC FRIDAY
Enthusiasm and Drive

I first discovered that I possessed drive when I was in engineering school at Kettering University. At the end of my freshman year, I was struggling. I felt out of place. I was away from my home in Alabama. I had no friends or family in Michigan. I began lacking confidence, and my grades were suffering accordingly. I was just about ready to give up.

That's when another treasured mentor, Dr. David Green, Jr., challenged me to fight for the goal of graduating. After his first talk with me, I developed an urge that morphed into an overwhelming desire to walk across that Kettering stage with my engineering degree in hand. I regularly envisioned the moment, and even attended graduation ceremonies that semester to motivate me further.

In May 1993, I not only lived out my vision, but I graduated with top grades and the honor of outstanding thesis. It was a major accomplishment. Even today, completing engineering school was the hardest thing I've ever done, greater than my master's degrees or earning my doctorate.

Dr. Green ignited my drive to achieve more than what I could see, feel, or even do on my own. He drilled me to believe in the gifts and talents God had given me. I'll never forget what he told me as he mentored me: "You can't regain lost time." That statement changed my life. It made me look at time as my most important commodity, realizing that I only have so much of it allocated to me and that I need to make the most of it with enthusiasm and drive. I have been very productive since then, and now I am leading three different organizations because I don't waste time.

> "You can't regain lost time." That statement changed my life.

Psychologists identify drive as an innate, determined urge to attain a goal or satisfy a need. It creates an insatiable appetite to become what you desire to be. The key ingredient to supporting and sustaining such drive in your life is enthusiasm. Defined as an intense and eager enjoyment, interest, or approval, enthusiasm creates a strong feeling of excitement about something that results in an absorbing, controlling possession of your mind by that interest. Enthusiasm causes eagerness, energy, zeal, and gusto.

My sophomore year at Kettering was a turning point in my life—thanks to discovering my enthusiasm. It was two weeks into the first semester that I was elected president of the Black Unity Congress. As you read earlier, it took considerable time and effort for me to convince the BUC to get behind my vision to no longer be a segregated organization. The school was less than five percent African American, so we had to become more inclusive to drive up membership and increase our impact in assisting and mentoring students.

As I took on that challenge, I got so excited to lead the way. Enthusiasm welled up within me, infusing me to be a true, selfless servant leader. It was not about me. It was all about the cause of serving and helping others. We got more involved with the student body, developed a mentorship program with area churches, and sat in on the school's President's Council for the first time. Our funding surged. Being a servant leader became a controlling possession that still absorbs me today.

Author and father of the power of positive thinking, Norman Vincent Peale, rightly stated that "enthusiasm spells the difference between mediocrity and accomplishment."[24] Writer and teacher J.D. Crighton added, "Enthusiasm is highly contagious, so what are you waiting for? Contaminate your students."[25]

Enthusiasm that fuels your drive can make all the difference on Friday when the long workweek is nearing its end, the weekend beckons, and you need that final push to not only get to the finish line, but to cross it ahead of the pack.

· · · · · · ·

Five attributes of a Fantastic Friday

Enthusiasm and drive will be your end-of-the-week companions as you allow this quintet of attributes to direct your attitude and your actions.

1. I'm fired up to be a part! When you can see yourself as being essential to doing something worthwhile, it gets you going.

When Rosina Hernandez was in college, she attended a rock concert at which one young man was brutally beaten by another. No one made an attempt to stop the beating. The next day, she was struck dumb to learn that the youth had died as a result of the pounding. Yet neither she, nor anyone else, had raised a hand to help him.

She could never forget the incident or her responsibility as an inactive bystander.

Some years later, Rosina saw another catastrophe. A car driving in the rain ahead of her suddenly skidded and plunged into a bay. The car landed head down in the water with only the tail end showing. In a moment, a woman appeared on the surface, shouting for help and saying her husband was stuck inside.

This time Rosina waited for no one. She plunged into the water, tried unsuccessfully to open the car door, then pounded on the back window as other bystanders stood on the causeway and watched. First, she screamed at them, begging for help, then cursed them, telling them there was a man dying in the car.

First one man, then another, finally dived into the water to assist Rosina. Together, they broke the safety glass and dragged the man out. They were just in time. A few minutes later it would have been all over.

The woman thanked Rosina for saving her husband, and Rosina was elated, riding an emotional high that lasted for weeks. She had promised herself that she would never again fail to do anything she could to save a human life—and she had made good on her promise.[26]

What project for your family or initiative at work can you become so fired up about that you'll stop at nothing to see it through?

2. Go knock it out! Sometimes, just getting something done is its own reward. My son, Joshua, encouraged us to upgrade to a programmable lighting system at our church. That required installing three new trusses in the ceiling and over 30 new lights on the trio of trusses. It was no small undertaking, and he wanted me to help. I looked at it as an opportunity to spend time with my incredibly smart and managerial son. We worked several days into the midnight hours to complete the task, but after it was finished, I felt such an incredible feeling. Together, my son and I had knocked it out!

3. It's great to be a part of this movement! History is filled with movements that made a world-changing difference for communities, nations, and humankind. In the United States alone, five come to mind.

The Boston Tea Party of 1773 was the first significant act of independence by American colonists against the British. The Women's Suffrage Parade in Washington D.C. in March 1913 took place on the eve of President Woodrow Wilson's inauguration and sparked other movements that finally led to the nineteenth amendment, which granted women the right to vote in 1920. The March on Washington for Jobs and Freedom in 1963 brought us Dr. Martin Luther King's iconic "I Have a Dream" speech and spurred the civil rights movement. The Stonewall Protests of 1969 propelled the LGBTQ+ community forward, and the Occupation of Alcatraz from 1969-1971 led to a new national policy of self-determination for Native Americans.

Movements can lead to positive and sweeping change, so why not view your key personal and professional goals the same way? My involvement and leadership in the Black Unity Congress became a movement for inclusivity. What is happening in your life that can make a difference both now and in the future?

4. This is an incredible opportunity! Opportunity is defined as a set of circumstances that make it *possible* to do something that's never been done before, even out of tragedy. The Irish Potato Famine (1846-1851) resulted in a 30 percent drop in the population of western Ireland. The prolonged suffering of the Irish peasantry broke survivors in both body and spirit.

John Bloomfield, the owner of Castle Caldwell in County Fermanagh, was working on the recovery of his estate when he noticed that the exteriors of his tenant farmers' small cottages had a vivid white finish. He was informed that there was a clay deposit on his property of unusually fine quality. To generate revenue and provide employment on his estate, he built a pottery in the village of Belleek in 1857. The unusually fine clay yielded a porcelain china that was translucent with a glass-like finish.

It was worked into traditional Irish designs and was an immediate success. Belleek's iridescent pearlized glaze has been enthusiastically purchased the world over.[27] A multimillion-dollar industry rose from innovative thinking during some very troubling times. What amazing opportunities await you at home or at work?

5. This moment is huge! You've surely heard the exhortation, "Be in the moment!" But how often are we actually there and ready to respond? When I was 16, I went to work as a lifeguard after completing six weeks of grueling, intense training that tested my mental, emotional, and physical discipline. As I began my first shift at the deepest end of the pool, I climbed up the ladder to take my seat—and saw through the water the wavering image of a little boy at the bottom of the pool. "Save him!" someone yelled.

I had trained precisely for that moment! My heart rate shot up and normal protocol went out the door. I was supposed to have blown my whistle three short times before acting. Instead, I dove into the water with my shirt on and my whistle still around my neck. Then I swam to the bottom, and brought the boy to the surface, placing him beside the pool. He was breathing and very scared, and I instantly let him know that he was safe before carrying him to a vending area for food and water. The moment was as huge as it gets, and my heart was just as large with joy!

A difference maker

There is nothing more inspiring to your enthusiasm and drive than knowing that you are making a difference in the lives of those around you—especially on a Friday. These four characteristics will help you do just that.

Impart confidence to other people.

In his book, *The Quest for Character*, Charles Swindoll told the story of when Dr. Daniel Boorstin of the Library of Congress spoke of five items that were in President Abraham Lincoln's pockets the night he was assassinated in April of 1865. Included were several old and worn newspaper articles. "The clippings," said Boorstin, "were concerned with the great deeds of Abraham Lincoln. One of them actually reports a speech by John Bright which says that Abraham Lincoln is 'one of the greatest men of all times.'"

The world now knows that Bright, a British statesman, was correct in his assessment of Lincoln, but in 1865, millions of people shared quite a different opinion. Lincoln's critics were fierce and many, even as the president agonized over the suffering and turmoil of his country being ripped to shreds by hatred and Civil War. There is something touchingly poignant about the thought of this great leader seeking confidence and self-assurance from a few old newspaper clippings.[28]

Everyone needs confidence. Make each Friday a day that you impart confidence to at least one other person.

Infuse hope in others.
In the late 1990s, I had the opportunity to infuse hope into a great guy. Keith was my classmate in high school, and he had fallen into a severe drug addiction. Late one evening, his sister asked me to go to the home of a friend he was staying with to encourage him not to give up on his life. I went and stood with Keith under the stars in the backyard, listening as he told me his story. It was one filled with hurt and disappointment.

My heart filled with compassion, and I began to paint a picture of what his future could look like if he made the decision to change his life. "Are you ready to change?" I asked.

I will never forget the look of expectation in Keith's eyes as he responded, "Yes, I am."

I knew he was serious, and I affirmed, "You are telling the truth."

Right there, Keith got down on his knees in the grass and repented to God. He later told me that my statement of confirmation gave him the confidence and drive he needed to move forward. Today, he runs a drug recovery program at our church and is doing great things.

Keep pushing forward.
Sometimes we can get excited about a project but then have that enthusiasm challenged by unforeseen circumstances. Such was the case for me in 2002 when I was taking the lead to organize a Christian minister's conference. We planned for months in advance, calling potential speakers, getting volunteers, and marketing the event. Then, just one week before the conference,

we had to move to a completely new venue because of a scheduling error for the original location.

Panic could've set in, but I knew that we had to keep calm, figure out a plan to relocate the conference, and get the word out to our speakers, volunteers, and attendees. We had to clean the new location's classrooms and rearrange several event activities there, but we pushed forward, allowing no excuses that we couldn't get it done. We pulled it off, and the conference turned out to be a great success.

Recondition the mind to accept the creative thought "climate."

Climate, as most of us think of it, refers to the long-term pattern of weather in a particular area. Weather can change from day-to-day, month-to-month, or even year-to-year. A region's weather patterns, usually tracked for at least 30 years, are considered its climate.

Now think of your brain. The long-term pattern of your thoughts, decisions, and actions makes up the climate of your life. A wise adage declares, "As a man thinks, so is he." How can you transform your thinking to stimulate the creativity and inventiveness you need to bring renewed enthusiasm and drive to your life? It'll likely start with dedicating more time for learning and personal development which takes you out of your comfort zone and stretches you mentally. Beyond that, what can you do to encourage those around you to change the climate of their thinking to become more creative?

> A wise adage declares, "As a man thinks, so is he."

• • • • • • •

Parting principles to head into the weekend

Even in this day of flexible schedules that depart from the traditional workweek model, the cry of "TGIF!" remains. There's still just something about Friday that let's you know that a welcome reprieve is coming. These eight principles of a Fantastic Friday will help you enter into that time informed and energized.

1. Enthusiasm is caught, not taught, through relationships: I caught the enthusiasm I needed to start motivational speaking one evening during a financial conference at the Von Braun Center in Huntsville. It was there, inside a packed arena filled with 10,000 people, that I first saw and heard the great Zig Ziglar. He delivered a keynote called Living Your Dream about going forward and getting out of your comfort zone. It was electrifying, and his energy was so compelling that I was preoccupied for days afterward thinking of how I could motivate people to be their best. I left that event telling myself, "I can do that. I know I can! I've just got to work on some things to get there." I was ready to go and empower others to change the world!

2. Drive is the essential ingredient to success: The late politician and educator Mark Hatfield told of touring Calcutta, India with Mother Teresa and visiting the places where sick children were cared for in their last days and the dispensary where the poor lined up by the hundreds to receive medical attention. As he watched Mother Teresa feeding and nursing those left behind by others, Hatfield was overwhelmed by the sheer magnitude of the suffering she and her co-workers faced daily. "How can you bear the load without being crushed by it?" he asked.

Mother Teresa replied, "My dear senator, I am not called to be successful. I am called to be faithful."[29]

Mother Teresa was driven by her calling, and her success was shown in how she helped others who were helpless. Allow whatever it is that drives you to empower you to succeed both personally and professionally.

3. Without enthusiasm, we are scarcely willing to endure the self-discipline and endless toil that is necessary to develop professional skill: When I started the 18-month program to earn my graduate certificate in business from Vanderbilt University, I was plenty enthusiastic about it—but I was promoted to chief operating officer of Ability Plus during that same time period. I knew that the program was going to be very beneficial to me, but it wasn't going to be easy, especially while maintaining my new professional responsibilities.

Therefore, I had to engage a higher level of self-discipline into my daily routine. About halfway through the program at Vanderbilt, one of the classes, Executive Leadership, was particularly demanding. It had more than the normal amount of homework and a special project as well. I knew I had no time to spare. It took some supreme discipline to keep up with it all, but I did it, and it was worth it. I'm still using the skills I developed during that program.

4. Drive is the dynamic motivator that keeps us persistently working toward our goals: In the spring of 1883, two young men graduated from medical school. They differed from one another in both appearance and ambition. Ben was short and stocky. Will was tall and thin. Ben dreamed of practicing medicine on the East Coast. Will wanted to work in a rural community. Ben begged his friend to go to New York with him, believing they could both make a fortune there, but Will refused.

His friend thought he was foolish for wanting to practice medicine in the Midwest. "But," Will insisted, "I want first of all to be a great surgeon, the very best, if I have the ability."

Years later, the wealthy and powerful came from around the world to be treated by Will at his clinic: the Mayo Clinic.[30] Will's foremost goal was not to pursue wealth, but to be great at what he did. That was the motivation that drove him—and his reward was more than he could've imagined. Let your drive propel you toward what will make you truly great!

5. Enthusiasm informs our future: During his 1960 presidential campaign, John F. Kennedy often closed his speeches with the story of Colonel Davenport, the former speaker of the Connecticut House of Representatives. Kennedy told of one day in 1789 when the skies over the city of Hartford darkened ominously, and some of the representatives, glancing out the windows, feared the end was at hand. Among the clamor, Davenport rose and said, "The Day of Judgment is either approaching or it is not. If it is not, there is no cause for adjournment. If it is, I choose to be found doing my duty. Therefore, I wish that candles be brought."[31]

Rather than being afraid of what is to come, we are to be faithful to the job at hand. The future is not to be feared. It is to be enthusiastically embraced as the opportunity that it is—for it is that very enthusiasm that affects and dictates how you face the days ahead.

> The future is not to be feared.

6. Drive affects our outlook on life: My drive to be the best I can be has been a constant positive force in my life—particularly when it comes to having influence in my community. I didn't pursue that influence to feel important or become popular. I did it to fulfill a calling on my life to help people reach their maximum potential.

Truth is, though, many people will not hear you or give any value to what you have to say if they feel you are not influential.

So, I have successfully been appointed to several boards of influence in the community, allowing me to move the needle in several areas including education, health, and finance. Through my influence with these organizations, positive change has occurred with ethnic minorities being given greater opportunities to better help their businesses, contribute, and help others. It's gone beyond basic diversity and inclusion efforts, and we've seen tremendous results.

7. Enthusiasm affects our influence on others to progress: When musician Pablo Casals reached the age of 95, a young reporter asked him a question. "Mr. Casals, you are the greatest cellist that ever lived. Why do you still practice six hours a day?"

Casals' answer: "Because I think I'm making progress."[32]

Truly great people never think they're great enough. They are always enthusiastic to progress and improve. Can you imagine the impact Casals had on young musicians as they watched the elder genius practice his craft? What about the impact you can have on others as you influence them to become more than they are right now?

8. Drive affects our commitment: There's a saying I've heard that I absolutely love, even if it is grammatically incorrect. "To succeed in life, you need not only initiative, but also finishiative."[33] We need to have the mindset of a finisher!

One year I oversaw a kid's summer camp project at my church, and I had the vision and drive to make it the best summer camp in the entire Huntsville area. We did not want to exclude anyone. Yet we hit one roadblock after another. Sponsors bailed out. Volunteers were not able to keep or complete their commitments. We wouldn't be deterred. We even did a special program where kids participated in building an actual go-kart that looked like a little Hummer. One of our elders was a mechanic who was very creative, and he led the charge.

The camp was an amazing success. The smiles from the kids were everything to us! When we took everyone to the Civil Rights Museum in Birmingham, Alabama, one of the children had never been outside our area or to the big city. It blew him away, and it expanded what he felt like he could do in life.

....

It's been quite a journey so far, hasn't it? From Sunday through Friday, we've learned how vision, attitude, belief, potential, confidence, and now enthusiasm and drive can feed one off the other and combine to send you soaring through your week with *No Bad Days*. But where does it all lead? To a Successful Saturday, of course, and the final element you need: purpose.

[7]

SUCCESSFUL SATURDAY
Purpose

Dr. Martin Luther King, Jr. surely said it best. "I submit to you that if a man hasn't discovered something he will die for, he isn't fit to live." Dr. Myles Munroe followed up nicely when he declared, "The only thing worse than death is life without purpose."

I've often told people that if they chase passion and purpose, then money, and everything else they desire, will find them. In the opening pages of this book, I wrote about knowing your "why"—the reason you exist: your purpose for living. I'll repeat it here: When you discover your why, you will search diligently to recognize how to accomplish it, and you will wait as long as it takes to gain the knowledge, stability, and experience to fulfill it.

My "why," or purpose for living, is to educate, equip, and empower people to reach their destiny by helping them to maximize their potential. That sounds great, and it is, but I didn't discover it automatically. I had to ask myself five questions of the heart—queries originally introduced by Dr. Munroe that will absolutely change your life and position you for ongoing success Saturday and every day.

Let's take a deeper dive into each one.

Heart question #1. Who am I?

This speaks to your identity. Many people want to be something that they are not, but we must be honest with ourselves and come to know who we are not—and who we are. This requires looking at our talents and gifts to determine what gives us energy and moves us in a positive direction.

> We must be honest with ourselves and come to know who we are not—and who we are.

It was in 2002 that I had a serious talk with myself. I was in my office at church and working in full-time ministry as a pastor. We had just purchased a new building and were doing alright, but we had been through some struggles, and I was at a crossroads. At the core of my dilemma was a simple question: "Am I supposed to be doing this?"

I had friends who were running companies. Several of my former college classmates were doing well and producing products. They were achieving more things, had more money, and were getting more accolades, and that frustrated me. I felt left out. I was an engineer at General Motors. Yet I was stuck speaking to a hundred people every week at a church, and it seemed to me that I wasn't moving fast enough at all. *What was I doing being some ordinary preacher?* I mused. *I don't want to be an ordinary preacher.*

I discovered that morning that I actually didn't want to be like my friends or continue comparing myself to them based on their fame or the income they earned. I resolved that I didn't want to be a person who did what I did just for notoriety or for money. From then on, I made some changes. As a pastor, I began altering how I preached and taught to broaden my influence and increase the outreach impact of the church. Professionally, I put everything into motion that led to what I am doing today. I ceased comparing myself to others and engaged my gifts in leadership.

Essentially, I defined who I was, what I wanted to do, and why I wanted to do it at my heart level.

Heart question #2. Where am I from?
This speaks to your source. We must determine the wellspring of our passion and our position. Are they birthed from the books we read, the people we are around, a power higher than ourselves, or all of the above?

I was always a pretty smart guy, but I determined at General Motors that I was not going to rely on myself or my wits as the source of my promotion. My sources were going to be God, mentorship, and reading books on purpose and personal development, not just what I thought was best for me. I recognized that God had given me direction and the callings for my life, and I was going to constantly train, learn, and grow. I also went to several seminars offered by the company and outside groups.

As I acted intentionally and focused my mindset, I defined where I was from by identifying my sources and using them for education and inspiration.

Heart question #3. Why am I here?
This speaks to your purpose. It is essential to know why we exist. This includes a consideration of why we live in a certain area, why we move in certain circles, and why we are spurred to action by certain things.

This question is not answered overnight. It took me until I was 37 years of age to properly answer it. I had chased status and riches, subscribing to a few multilevel marketing companies in the process, in hopes of earning lots of money before I came to the conclusion that my purpose was to help people maximize their potential.

The answer came during my second trip to Nigeria. My first visit was solely to take part in an evangelical crusade, but this time I also conducted a leadership seminar under Dr. Timothy Ifedioranma. I felt energy and passion as I made my presentation, and I witnessed the positive effect it had on the participants. Not only were they excited, but they also asked some really tough questions. "Can you pastor and own a business?" "How do you lead in the business world versus the pastor's world?" They wanted to know more about what I did and when I was coming back.

That's when I knew that helping others maximize their potential defined the very heart of what I wanted to do.

Heart question #4. What can I do?

This speaks to your potential. We must ask ourselves what we can do in this world to "move the needle." That's a term that has been around for quite a while and calls to mind the volume gauge on an old radio or the needle on the speedometer of a classic car. Simply defined, to move the needle is to "change a situation to a noticeable degree." What gift do we possess that can do this? Do we need to work harder, stay up later, or get up earlier to make it happen?

In 2011, I decided to live to my greatest potential. More specifically, I told myself I was going to "live full and die empty." I was in my early forties at the time, looking ahead to my fifties, and I was just beginning my leadership role at Ability Plus. I was chief operations officer then, and I observed that my style of leadership was having an impact on our employees, particularly those who had never before experienced leadership training. When I was all in, they were all in, and it caused them to head in a positive direction.

From then on, I started volunteering to serve on more director's boards and mentoring others even as I was being mentored. I also launched the API Institute of Leadership and Development, which offered seminars and training sessions to assist others in reaching their potential. I did it because I knew I needed to help them. API students still text, email, and write me about what they are doing and how they are helping others because of the leadership and direction I sowed into them.

I tell people that my plan is to work as hard as I can until I'm about 65 and then start backing off and enjoying other things. Whatever I do, work or leisure, I want to do it with my whole heart. When I close my eyes for good someday and go home to be with the Lord, I don't want to carry anything with me. I want to leave everything behind as a legacy to others.

Heart question #5. Where am I going?

This speaks to your destiny. What does the future look like?

Raised in government housing, I had to see beyond my neighborhood. Even as a kid, I saw people around me settling for less. When teenagers graduated from school, they might have gotten a job, but they weren't going to college or anywhere else. They stayed in the neighborhood. Some eventually got in trouble. Many adults didn't work, and it seemed that those who did weren't trying to advance in life. Mediocrity was fine with them.

I didn't want any of that. I couldn't imagine being in my thirties and still living in a place, and in a system, where I had to do everything I could just to have food and housing.

There had to be more.

In fifth grade, I made a decision: I was going to be successful. I looked into the future and saw a destiny where I owned a house and a car, ran businesses, and changed the world. I didn't know or understand how any of that would take place. I just envisioned it on the canvas of my imagination.

I did know that I was going to have to work hard and get good grades in school to make it possible, so I started applying myself and studying—and two teachers made an amazing difference that year. The first was Ms. O'Shields. She was my math teacher, and she recognized early on that I had a high math IQ. In her wisdom, she told me to work at my own speed, and I finished the math book in one semester. I became a tutor to the other kids, and she gave me other math to do that was more advanced and not in the textbook.

Ms. O'Shields rewarded me by driving me home from school in her small, yellow sports car, often stopping for ice cream along the way. We went to the Dairy Queen on Moulton Street, and I always got a Peanut Buster Parfait! As we sat together inside the ice cream shop, Ms. O'Shields spoke into my life, insisting that I could be whatever I wanted to be. I was just a boy, but she was a mentor and encourager.

The second was my science teacher, Mrs. Scott. She was one of those teachers who was very disciplined and demanded the same from her pupils. Every Thursday was test day, and if anyone failed, they got a paddling on Friday. I know that sounds very old school and even abusive today, but back then it was the norm. Students who routinely failed wore two pairs of pants to lessen the sting of the paddling, hoping their name wasn't going to be called.

One Friday early in the year, she called *my* name. I was such a good student the whole class almost stopped breathing. So did I.

I was the last person she paddled that day. "I failed the test?" I asked, confused.

"No," she said. "I already talked to your mom. You had an 89. You don't make 89s. You make 99s in my class. You are capable of that."

I never got paddled again.

Ms. O'Shields and Mrs. Scott set the stage for me to go on, get a scholarship and sponsorship to attend Kettering University, and excel as an adult. I didn't stay in the neighborhood. I did not settle for mediocrity. In my heart, I knew where I was going—and I got there!

* * * * * * *

Typically, Saturday is a day to get things done that you couldn't take care of Monday-Friday. Of course, being Saturday, you may not want to do those things. After all, the weekend has arrived. It's time to chill a bit, right?

So, to help you stay productive yet relaxed, Saturday comes with a couple of attributes to do just that.

Saturday is a source of enthusiasm.

Dr. Norman Vincent Peale is quoted in "The Power of Positive Thinking" as writing, "Apathy can only be overcome by enthusiasm, and enthusiasm can only be aroused by two things; first, an ideal which takes the imagination by storm, and second, a definite intelligible plan for carrying that ideal into practice."

Enthusiasm is a mental position of victory along the marathon course of your week. In their original Olympic Games, the Greeks had a race that was unique. In it, the winner was not the runner who finished first. It was the runner who finished with his torch still lit.[34] An excitement and fervor to do your tasks for the day, combined with a plan to get it done, will keep your flame burning and propel you to achieve some incredible things. When asked for the secret behind his amazing achievements, Sir Edward V. Appleton, the Scottish physicist whose scientific discoveries made possible worldwide broadcasting and won him a Nobel prize, said it was enthusiasm. "I rate enthusiasm even above professional skill."[35]

> Enthusiasm is a mental position of victory along the marathon course of your week.

Author Irving Stone spent a lifetime studying greatness, writing novelized biographies of such men as Michelangelo and Vincent van Gogh. Stone was once asked if he had found a thread that runs through the lives of all these exceptional people. His response was enlightening.

"I write about people who sometime in their life...have a vision or dream of something that should be accomplished... and they go to work. They are beaten over the head, knocked down, vilified, and for years they get nowhere. But every time they're knocked down, they stand up. You cannot destroy these people. And at the end of their lives, they've accomplished some modest part of what they set out to do."[36]

What can you do, using the many suggestions from earlier in *No Bad Days*, to foster enthusiasm on Saturday?

Saturday is the womb of perseverance.

Perseverance is having steady persistence in spite of difficulties or obstacles. On Saturday, this usually means pushing through and getting it done when distractions come upon you. It can also require you to overcome discouragement from others.

Even the greatest personalities have been told they wouldn't persevere or succeed. Former British statesman and prime minister Winston Churchill seemed so dull as a youth that his father thought he might be incapable of even earning a living in England. Writer and theologian G.K. Chesterton could not read until he was eight. One of his teachers cruelly told him, "If we could open your head, we should not find any brain but only a lump of white fat." Inventor Thomas Edison's first teacher described him as "addled," and his father almost convinced him he was a dunce. Theoretical physicist Albert Einstein, whose very name is synonymous with genius, performed so badly in all high school courses except mathematics that a teacher asked him to drop out.[37]

I'm so glad Ms. O'Shields and Mrs. Scott weren't like those teachers. Comments like this would have destroyed my perseverance before it could be birthed and grown.

The booklet *Bits & Pieces* shared an interesting story about Florence Chadwick, the first woman to swim the English Channel in both directions. Way back on the Fourth of July in 1951, she attempted to swim from Catalina Island to the California coast. The challenge was not so much the distance, but the bone-chilling waters of the Pacific. To complicate matters, a dense fog lay over the entire area, making it impossible for her to see land.

After about 15 hours in the water, and within just a half mile of her goal, Chadwick gave up. Later she told a reporter,

"Look, I'm not excusing myself. But if I could have seen land, I might have made it."

Not long afterward she attempted the feat again. Once more, a misty veil obscured the coastline, and she couldn't see the shore. But this time she made it because she kept reminding herself that land was there. With that confidence, she bravely swam on and achieved her goal. In fact, she broke the men's record by over two hours![38]

What can you apply from our earlier lessons on visualization each Saturday to create perseverance in your life each weekend?

* * * * * * *

Purposeful traits for a Successful Saturday

Eight is great, or so it is said—and over the years, I have identified and practiced eight traits that are ideal for nurturing direction and purpose on Saturday that will provide a foundation for your daily success.

Interestingly, each one requires selflessness and intentionality.

1. Clearly communicate your vision and performance expectations.

On Saturday morning, I get up, make a cup of coffee, have a time of devotion reflecting on God's goodness, then go over my vision. As I do this each week, I look back at what was accomplished to get me that much closer to achieving the milestones and goals of the overall vision. One such morning in June 2019, I started my Successful Saturday routine and discovered that I was not putting enough focus on self-discipline. I was taking part in too many nonproductive meetings.

So, I began streamlining my schedule to get rid of meetings that did not positively feed the future of the overall vision. Since then, I am more productive. I don't have wasted time. I look at my schedule, discern what is truly needed, and tell my administrative assistant to decline what's left. I've gotten to the place where I can ask somebody else in our organization to handle those meetings without feeling guilty about it. It's taken a while, but I've learned the power of delegation and the freedom that comes from saying "no." I can pass it on or refuse it, and it's okay.

Remove any and all distractions, then review your vision weekly, communicate it again to yourself, and do whatever is necessary to fulfill it.

2. Make lightning-fast decisions.

It's proper to take some time to ruminate and deliberate, but when the time for action arrives, stop thinking and go on.

An often-used quote for business and inspiration states that while an open mind is priceless, "it is priceless only when its owner has the courage to make a final decision which closes the mind for action after the process of viewing all sides of the question has been completed. Failure to make a decision after due consideration of all the facts will quickly brand a man as unfit for a position of responsibility."

It concludes, "Not all of your decisions will be correct. None of us is perfect. But if you get into the habit of making decisions, experience will develop your judgment to a point where it is better to be right fifty percent of the time and get something done, than it is to get nothing done because you fear to reach a decision."[39]

Don't allow anxiety or concern to make you indecisive. Have confidence in your acquired wisdom and trust your instincts. Act—then proactively respond to whatever comes next.

3. Put the spotlight on others.

Many times, it's easy to feel like no one is noticing what we're doing—but really, it's all about telling someone else's story anyway. I'm a big college football fan. On fall and winter Saturdays, ESPN's College GameDay spotlights athletes who have overcome adversity or done outstanding things for others and the communities where they play. These features go beyond the game and spotlight worthy young men and women.

Saturday is a great day for you to shine a light on somebody else just like ESPN does. That's why I usually call someone on my staff and tell them, "You know what so-and-so is doing? Let me tell you!" I declare how that individual has gone above and beyond to other leaders on my team. Many times, the person I feature is doing things others are not even aware of. In late 2022, I talked about a worker at Ability Plus who routinely went far above and beyond his job description to recruit other workers or volunteers to assist in the homes he was overseeing, particularly during a time when we were severely short staffed. He took it upon himself to maintain and improve the quality of care we offer our clients. He even took his residents on a special outing once he knew he had secured proper and safe supervision for the excursion.

When you recognize and celebrate the success of others, it gives you a sense of fulfillment and even victory. When you see others who are winning, it opens your mind to doing the same thing yourself. It's a win-win for everyone!

4. Put yourself last.

Every young student knows of Isaac Newton's famed encounter with a falling apple. Newton discovered and introduced the laws of gravity in the 1600s, which revolutionized astronomical studies. But few know that if it weren't for Edmund Halley, the world might never have learned from Newton.

It was Halley who challenged Newton to think through his original notions. Halley corrected Newton's mathematical errors and prepared geometrical figures to support his discoveries. Halley coaxed the hesitant Newton to write his great work, *Philosophiæ Naturalis Principia Mathematica,* or Mathematical Principles of Natural Philosophy, first published in Latin in 1687. It was Halley who edited and supervised the publication and financed its printing even though Newton was wealthier and could have afforded the printing costs.

Historians still refer to it as one of the most selfless examples in the annals of science. Newton began to reap the rewards of prominence almost immediately, and Halley received little credit. However, he did use the principles to predict the orbit and return of the comet that would later bear his name, but it was only after his death that Halley received any acclaim—and because the comet only returns to earth every 76 years, the notice is rather infrequent. Halley remained a devoted scientist who didn't care who received the credit as long as the cause was being advanced.[40]

Advancement solely for the sake of self is never a trait of a successful person. Use your gifts and talents to their fullest and to attain the greatest, regardless of recognition.

> Use your gifts and talents to their fullest and to attain the greatest.

5. Accept full responsibility and share the credit.

We must accept the fact that 100 percent of what happens to us, or in the spaces where we lead, is our responsibility. This is true no matter how much or how little we can control and whether or not we win or lose. In addition, when triumphs occur, we should always share the credit with our team and anyone else who contributed to the victory. When we landed a new client, the University of Alabama at Birmingham Health Systems, to receive coaching and leadership training, I told my team that it happened because of all of their efforts. It was not because of Doc Rock. My name is up front, yes, but it is everyone else's hard work that resulted in the research and negotiating that secured the client. I credited them and rewarded them.

Conversely, when we fail, we must accept the fault as our own. When I made strategic changes in how the ministry and outreach of my church was conducted, we lost many people. They decided to go elsewhere, and that had a negative impact on our revenue and our morale. At one point, it appeared we may have to close our doors entirely. I was the leader. I took the blame. I took responsibility for it. I could've blamed some of the members and volunteers at the church, but I put it on me and told everyone I was going to correct it. I asked people to keep following and believing in our leadership. The strategic changes I made weren't wrong, and they weren't a failure. It was a transition that temporarily had negative consequences. Then, when things turned around, I gave credit to those who made it possible.

Never shirk your responsibility and never think you're the only one running the show. Have the tenacity and courage to truly lead.

SUCCESSFUL SATURDAY – PURPOSE

6. Keep people on their toes.

Newspaper editor Arthur Brisbane was overheard telling his best cartoonist, Windsor McKay, that he was the second greatest cartoonist in the world. Curiosity aroused, a reporter standing nearby asked Brisbane who was first.

"I don't know," he replied. "But it keeps McKay on his toes."[41]

Keeping others on their toes is simply the art of encouraging someone to take those few more steps to get to greatness. Many times on Saturday, I will take the time to ask one of my leaders if they have maximized their potential. Is there another step they can take on the ladder? Are they sure they are reaching for their best? Most of them thank me later for stretching them beyond what they thought was the maximum they could achieve.

One of our church leaders volunteers in our technology department, and he faced a huge personal challenge when we converted from an analog control board to a digital one for the building's audio, video, web services, and lighting. He was accustomed to the analog equipment and uncomfortable with learning the newer and more complex computerized system. "I'm going to need some help," he pleaded with me. "I don't know these computers."

I replied, "You can do it. It is in you. The skill set is already there. Now is the time to develop it like never before." He agreed to try. He failed a few times at first, but he persevered. Before long, he ran the digital system as well as the old analog one. Lighting, audio, video, webcasting—he could do it all.

Challenge apathy and be willing to have yourself and those you lead take on new things. Keep everyone on their toes and encourage them along the way.

7. Take risks without being reckless.

In 1982, the ABC Evening News reported on an unusual work of modern art—a chair affixed to a shotgun. It was to be viewed by sitting in the chair and looking directly into the gun barrel. The gun was loaded and set on a timer to fire at an undetermined moment within the next 100 years.

The amazing thing was that people waited in lines to sit and stare into the shell's path! They all knew the gun could go off at point-blank range at any moment, but they were gambling that the fatal blast wouldn't happen during their minute in the chair.[42]

The risk they took with their lives was needless, but necessary risk is always a trait of a successful person. Former president Franklin D. Roosevelt once said, "It is common sense to take a method and try it. If it fails, admit it frankly. But above all, try something!" Failing to try because of a desire to be secure results in inaction.

John Henry Jowett, a great English preacher, likewise pointed out the temptation of self-preservation and its result in faithless lives. He said, "It is possible to evade a multitude of sorrows through the cultivation of an insignificant life. Indeed, if a man's ambition is to avoid the troubles of life, the recipe is simple: shed your ambitions in every direction, cut the wings of every soaring purpose, and seek a life with the fewest contacts and relations. If you want to get through the world with the smallest trouble, you must reduce yourself to the smallest compass. Tiny souls can dodge through life; bigger souls are blocked on every side. As soon as a man begins to enlarge his life, his resistances are multiplied."[43]

There is no reason to be timid or to diminish yourself. Take a chance, embrace calculated risk, and see what happens. A *No Bad Days* life is one that is fully lived!

8. Lead by example.
Writer Mark Twain humorously stated, "Few things are harder to put up with than the annoyance of a good example." When former United States Secretary of State, General George C. Marshall, took command of the infantry school at Fort Benning, Georgia, he found the post in a generally run-down condition. Rather than issue orders for specific improvements, he simply got out his own paintbrushes and lawn equipment and went to work on his personal quarters. The other officers and men, first on his block, then throughout the post, did the same thing, and Fort Benning was brightened up in no time.[44]

One particularly inspiring tale of example, especially when you consider its historical context, occurred in 1865. One Sunday morning, a black man entered a fashionable church in Richmond, Virginia. When Communion was served, he walked down the aisle and knelt at the altar.

A rustle of resentment swept through the congregation. How dare he! After all, believers in that church used the common cup.

Suddenly, a distinguished layman stood up, stepped forward to the altar, and knelt beside the black man. With Robert E. Lee setting the example, the rest of the congregation soon followed his lead.[45]

Being a good example to others often requires courage, but it is worth it. Each Saturday, examine how you can be a better example to your family, friends, and colleagues—then follow through on that the rest of the week.

Three principles of purpose

We've covered so much in *No Bad Days*, so it seems more than appropriate to close with three brief but incredible and foundational principles that will not only shine purpose into your Successful Saturdays, but every other day of the week as well.

Purpose is the master of motivation.

Motivation is the general desire or willingness to do something. An irresistible, consuming purpose will motivate you and will not let you go. Identify a purpose with goals that you've just got to reach. Then build toward those goals under the fire of anticipation.

Purpose is the mother of commitment.

Commitment is a deliberated and calculated choice to steadfastly set your course with an unwavering obligation to go above and beyond your original expectation to accomplish a predetermined objective.

Purpose gives birth to hope.

Hope is a feeling of expectation and desire for a certain thing to happen. Hope builds your self-confidence and inspires you to believe that you are capable of achieving great things by enabling yourself to aim higher and work smarter.

DON'T WAIT FOR TOMORROW!

As with most things in life, it all comes down to how you look at it.

Do you automatically think Monday will be a bad day, Wednesday will be a get-through-it sort of day, and Friday will be a great day? That's what most people tend to believe.

But that's just it: it's a belief based on a preconception. Therefore, if you begin to believe that every day will be a great day filled with productivity and joy—that there are indeed *No Bad Days*—guess what that does to your attitude? It transforms it!

That mindset change is essential, but it is not enough. You need to follow it up with action, and that is what *No Bad Days* empowers you to do. It gives you principles and calls to action that you can implement every day.

"Thank God it's Friday?" Maybe. But how about if you can start to say, "Thank God it's Monday, or Tuesday, or Wednesday"—or whatever day it is? There are opportunities in every day. No matter the circumstances, no matter how hard it is, and no matter how tough it seems, it doesn't make a difference! Why? You are not living for the weekend. You are living for each day as it comes!

What has writing and living *No Bad Days* done to me? It calls upon me to not wait for tomorrow to have joy. It calls upon me to approach every day with the idea that I can accomplish something. When I get up in the morning, it is the first day of the rest of my life! It forces me to maximize that day so that I can leave it all on the field and get the most out of it.

Tomorrow will take care of itself. It might have problems. It might have challenges. But I will not wait until tomorrow to experience my fullest life today!

Can you think of any better way to live than that?

ENDNOTES

1. Martin Luther King, Jr., "I Have A Dream: Writings and Speeches that Changed the World," ed. James Melvin Washington (San Francisco: Harper, 1986), pgs. 102-106.
2. Robert J. Morgan, Nelson's Annual Preacher's Sourcebook, 2002 Edition, (Thomas Nelson Inc., 2001), p.324.
3. https://theanguillian.com/2017/11/from-rags-to-riches-the-life-story-of-dr-myles-munroe-by-russel-reid/
4. "4 Stories About Work Ethic That Will Make You Work Harder," A.J. Agrawal, Inc.com, March 21, 2015.
5. "Researcher: Monday Funk All in the Mind," Chicago Tribune, July 2, 1997, sec. 1, pg. 8.
6. Let's Be: The power of thoughts. The Express, by Nancy Hackenberg, certified life coach and owner of Be One Healthy Fitness Center, Mill Hall, PA. https://www.lockhaven.com/news/health-and-home/2022/03/lets-be-the-power-of-thoughts/
7. https://www.researchgate.net/publication/276002060_Rosenberg_Self-Esteem_Scale_Greek_Validation_on_Student_Sample
8. www.brainyquotes.com.
9. www.famousquotes.com.
10. Learning to Lead, J.M. Boice, Revell, 1990, p. 38. Taken from http://www.sermonillustrations.com/
11. Bits and Pieces, September 19, 1991, p. 18. Taken from http://www.sermonillustrations.com/
12. Mike Lupica in Esquire. Taken from http://www.sermonillustrations.com/
13. Bits & Pieces, September 19, 1991, p. 9. Taken from http://www.sermonillustrations.com/
14. John McKay, "A Coach's Story." Taken from http://www.sermonillustrations.com/
15. https://kclpure.kcl.ac.uk/portal/robert.plomin.html
16. Courtesy Alkha Puranik, Setmycoach.com
17. From LifeQuoteslive.com
18. Source Unknown. Taken from http://www.sermonillustrations.com/

19 William C. Schultz, Bits & Pieces, December 1990.
    Taken from http://www.sermonillustrations.com/
20 Today in the Word, September 5, 1993.
    Taken from http://www.sermonillustrations.com/
21 Our Daily Bread. Taken from http://www.sermonillustrations.com/
22 Bits and Pieces, November, 1989, p. 21.
    Taken from http://www.sermonillustrations.com/
23 M. Littleton in Moody Monthly, June, 1989, p. 29.
    Taken from http://www.sermonillustrations.com/
24 http://www.quotefancy.com/
25 http://www.quoteslyfe.com/ and https://www.jdcrighton.com/about/
26 Bits & Pieces, June 24, 1993, pp. 20-21.
    Taken from http://www.sermonillustrations.com/
27 Bits and Pieces, June 25, 1992.
    Taken from http://www.sermonillustrations.com/
28 Swindoll, The Quest For Character, Multnomah, p. 62-3.
    Taken from http://www.sermonillustrations.com/
29 Beals, Beyond Hunger.
    Taken from http://www.sermonillustrations.com/
30 Today in the Word, July, 1990, p. 17.
    Taken from http://www.sermonillustrations.com/
31 Harry Heintz. Taken from http://www.sermonillustrations.com/
32 Dr. Maxwell Maltz, quoted in Bits & Pieces, June 24, 1993, p. 12. Taken from http://www.sermonillustrations.com/
33 Zaida Jones Blaine in Chicago Tribune.
    Taken from http://www.sermonillustrations.com/
34 J. Stowell, Fan The Flame, Moody, 1986, p. 32.
    Taken from http://www.sermonillustrations.com/
35 https://brandongaille.com/10-magnificent-edward-appleton-quotes/
36 Crossroads, Issue No. 7, p. 18.
    Taken from http://www.sermonillustrations.com/
37 Irving Wallace, Book of Lists, 1986, Wm. Morrow & Co., Ny, Ny. Taken from http://www.sermonillustrations.com/
38 Our Daily Bread. Taken from http://www.sermonillustrations.com/
39 Taken from http://www.sermonillustrations.com/
40 C.S. Kirkendall, Jr. Taken from http://www.sermonillustrations.com/
41 Bits & Pieces, January 7, 1993, p. 19.
    Taken from http://www.sermonillustrations.com/
42 Jeffrey D. King. Taken from http://www.sermonillustrations.com/
43 Paul Borthwick, Leading the Way, Navpress, 1989, p. 86.
    Taken from http://www.sermonillustrations.com/
44 Source Unknown. Taken from http://www.sermonillustrations.com/
45 Today in the Word, September, 1991, p. 15.
    Taken from http://www.sermonillustrations.com/

Made in the USA
Columbia, SC
26 January 2025